BrainRules

Medina

The
Purposeful
Classroom

www.fisherandfrey.com

youtube: fisherandfrey

Douglas Fisher
Nancy Frey

The
Purposeful
Classroom

How to Structure
Lessons with Learning
Goals in Mind

 Alexandria, Virginia USA

1703 N. Beauregard St. • Alexandria, VA 22311 1714 USA
Phone: 800-933-2723 or 703-578-9600 • Fax: 703-575-5400
Website: www.ascd.org • E-mail: member@ascd.org
Author guidelines: www.ascd.org/write

Gene R. Carter, *Executive Director*; Judy Zimny, *Chief Program Development Officer*;
Nancy Modrak, *Publisher*; Scott Willis, *Director, Book Acquisitions & Development*;
Julie Houtz, *Director, Book Editing & Production*; Ernesto Yermoli, *Editor*; Georgia Park,
Senior Graphic Designer; Mike Kalyan, *Production Manager*; Cynthia Stock, *Typesetter*;
Sarah Plumb, *Production Specialist*

Printed in the United States of America. Cover art © 2011 by ASCD. ASCD
publications present a variety of viewpoints. The views expressed or implied in this
book should not be interpreted as official positions of the Association.

All web links in this book are correct as of the publication date below but may have
become inactive or otherwise modified since that time. If you notice a deactivated or
changed link, please e-mail books@ascd.org with the words "Link Update" in the subject
line. In your message, please specify the web link, the book title, and the page number
on which the link appears.

PAPERBACK ISBN: 978-1-4166-1314-5   ASCD product #112007   n10/11

Also available as an e-book (see Books in Print for the ISBNs).

Quantity discounts for the paperback edition only: 10–49 copies, 10%; 50+ copies, 15%;
for 1,000 or more copies, call 800-933-2723, ext. 5634, or 703-575-5634. For desk copies:
member@ascd.org.

Library of Congress Cataloging-in-Publication Data
Fisher, Douglas, 1965–
  The purposeful classroom : how to structure lessons with learning goals in mind /
Douglas Fisher and Nancy Frey.
      p. cm.
  Includes bibliographical references and index.
  ISBN 978-1-4166-1314-5 (pbk. : alk. paper)
  1. Lesson planning. 2. Effective teaching. I. Frey, Nancy, 1959– II. Title.
  LB1027.4.F57 2011
  371.102—dc23

                                                                          2011025398

20 19 18 17 16 15 14 13 12 11   1 2 3 4 5 6 7 8 9 10 11 12

The Purposeful Classroom

How to Structure Lessons with Learning Goals in Mind

Acknowledgments

This book exists because Dr. John Nelson, instructional leader and Assistant Superintendent for the Chula Vista Elementary School District, asked us to clarify our thinking about establishing purpose. In doing so, we were honored to work with district and site leaders from the entire district, as well as the hundreds of teachers who served on their school's instructional leadership team during the 2009–2010 and 2010–2011 school years. They have provided feedback and ideas that have been incorporated into this book. Along the way, student achievement in the Chula Vista Elementary School District soared and more students than ever before reached proficiency.

We received very helpful feedback and advice from Dr. Page Dettmann, Executive Director of Middle Schools for the Sarasota Public School System, and her team, including Rob Manoogian, Sue Meckler, Deanne Nelson, and Judi Robson. Their efforts to implement the gradual release of responsibility have been enlightening for us and have allowed us an opportunity to refine our thinking. The students in Sarasota have benefited considerably from their work.

Dr. David Lorden, Assistant Superintendent in the San Diego Unified School District, allowed us to develop the self-assessment rubric found in Chapter 1 with his leadership team. David questioned each and every idea on the rubric and then worked to develop actionable plans for its use. In doing so, he introduced the principals in Area 8 to these ideas. This group of principals—Kathy Burns, Mary (Cathy) Calcagno, John (Brad) Callahan, Pat Crowder, E. Jay Derwae, Dave Downey, Bruce Ferguson, Judy Fogel, Elizabeth (Listy) Gillingham, Mike Jimenez, Stacy Jones, Jamie Jorgensen, Susan Levy, Yolanda Lewis, Jonathan McDade, Mary (Lorelei) Olsen, Bonnie Remington, Sarah Sullivan, and Kathy Wolfe—shared their thinking and made helpful suggestions about the ideas contained on the rubric and its implementation.

Also helpful was our experience at Health Sciences High & Middle College (HSHMC), where we work with students in grades 9–12. Every teacher at HSHMC has provided advice, guidance, examples, and support for our work. We are honored to call them colleagues and friends.

Finally, the skillful hand of Scott Willis has graced every one of our ASCD books, and we are pleased to count on his thinking and friendship as we attempt to share our experiences with others.

1

Establishing Purpose for Yourself and Your Students

"Great minds have purposes, others have wishes."

The author of this quote, Washington Irving, created the memorable character Rip Van Winkle. You may recall that Rip fell asleep one day and awoke 20 years later, confused about what had occurred and unable to make sense of his surroundings. Misadventures ensued as he failed to recognize his neighbors, confronted a man using his name (really his adult son), and announced his loyalty to the British throne, unaware that the American Revolution had been fought while he slept. Although Van Winkle was immersed in an environment that held all the clues he needed to understand his circumstances, he couldn't recognize them.

Otherwise effective classrooms sometimes operate this way, too. The cues that seem so obvious to us as teachers can be lost on students who, like Rip Van Winkle, fail to perceive the context and intent of what we're doing and what they should be learning. Good teachers work hard, using the latest in research-based practices and well-designed curriculum materials. But sometimes teachers rely a little too much on hope— hope that students will learn what we're teaching. Instead, we need to be clear about the purpose of every lesson.

Establishing Purpose

Establishing the purpose of a lesson, often through a written objective, is a common educational practice. From the time teachers get their professional licensure, they are encouraged to consider what their students will know and be able to do. An established purpose alerts learners to important information and garners their attention while helping teachers decide how best to use their instructional time. Consider the following content purpose statement:

> To identify the steps in the life cycle of a frog

After reading that statement, do you know what the teacher wants her students to learn? Could you identify instructional materials or plan instructional events that would help guide students' understanding? Could you identify an assessment that would reveal which students had mastered this information? Hopefully, your answer to each of these questions is "yes."

While we can improve the quality of the statement above, perhaps by increasing relevance or focusing on the linguistic demands of the lesson (elements that will be discussed further in this book), our point is that a clearly established purpose drives instruction. We don't ask students to infer the purpose; we clearly state it.

Purpose = Expectations

Establishing a clear purpose for learning content serves as a priming mechanism for new learning and results in increased student understanding of the content (Gagné & Briggs, 1974; Hunter, 1976; Mager, 1962). Simply put, when students understand the purpose of a lesson, they learn more (Fraser, Walberg, Welch, & Hattie, 1987).

In stating a purpose, we make our expectations for learning clear. When teachers have high expectations for students, communicate those expectations, and provide the support necessary to achieve them, student performance soars; conversely, when teachers have low expectations and communicate this either verbally or nonverbally, student achievement suffers (Marzano, 2011). Evidence from high-poverty schools in London, England, suggests that high expectations can also help reduce delinquency and behavioral disturbances (Rutter, Maughan, Mortimore, Ouston, & Smith, 1979). We also know that teachers' low expectations for students from traditionally underperforming groups contribute to the achievement gap (van den Bergh, Denessen, Hornstra, Voeten, & Holland, 2010).

One of the ways teachers can measure high expectations is by analyzing whether the stated purpose for learning content matches the grade level being taught. A simple review of the purpose statement will reveal lessons that are below grade level and thus not designed to ensure that students reach high expectations. After all, excellent teaching of 4th grade standards to 6th grade students will result, at best, in a group of 7th graders performing at the 5th grade level. That's not to say that a teacher would never provide students with some developmental instruction—closing knowledge and skills gaps is important, and can be accomplished during guided instruction. But lessons that are provided to the whole class, as well as the productive group work that students do collaboratively, should be aligned to grade-level expectations.

Objectives Versus Purpose Statements

A *lesson objective* is in the mind of the teacher; *establishing purpose* refers to the act of carefully communicating the objective to students. The establishment of purpose is accomplished through intentional use of lesson objectives by the teacher to let students know what they will learn and what they will be expected to do with what they've learned. A clearly stated and understood purpose lays the foundation for a schema building of concepts, skills, and information.

There are many excellent resources focused on writing lesson objectives (e.g., Mager, 1962; Marzano, 2009). We will touch on this subject in Chapter 2, but it is not the main focus of this book. We are interested in how the purpose of a lesson is communicated to students and how the established purpose guides learning. This requires more than writing a quality objective, which, though important, is insufficient to achieve the results we're after. We want students to become self-directed, motivated, critical thinkers who understand the world around them.

The terms *goals* and *objectives* have been used for decades to refer to broad categories of written or verbal statements that describe what students should learn in a given unit or lesson. Goals most often represent a larger curricular focus, while objectives represent smaller, more specific segments of learning that lead to the goal (Gronlund & Linn, 1990). For example, in special education, a goal on an Individual Education Program (IEP) typically encompasses a year of instruction, with stated objectives representing incremental benchmarks toward the goal (Billingsley, 1984). These objectives require that the time and evidence of learning be specified. The design of IEPs is influenced by the work of Mager (1962), who suggested that behavioral objectives (1) contain a measurable verb that describes the performance, (2) outline the conditions under which the objective is to be achieved, and (3) note the criteria for determining success.

However, as Marzano, Pickering, and Pollock (2001) explain, a narrowly defined objective can actually inhibit student performance because it "focuses students' attention to such a degree that they ignore information not specifically related to the goal" (p. 94). This effect can be especially troubling for teachers of English language learners, who are attempting to build schema by encouraging students to draw on their background knowledge and prior experiences. An overly narrow objective may result in students editing out such salient information.

"SMART" is a commonly used mnemonic device for helping people remember the components of a well-crafted objective. Originally, SMART stood for Specific, Measurable, Attainable, Relevant, and Time-based. However, it has been revised over time with additional words for added clarity. For example, Haughey (2010) suggests the following:

S - Specific, significant, stretching
M - Measurable, meaningful, motivational
A - Agreed-upon, attainable, achievable, acceptable, action-oriented
R - Realistic, relevant, reasonable, rewarding, results-oriented
T - Time-based, timely, tangible, trackable

As we will discuss in greater detail in Chapter 2, understanding the components of an effective *objective* is important in a teacher's planning process, whereas the *purpose* has to be understood by students such that they can explain it in their own words and grasp its relevance. In other words, teachers who painstakingly write objectives that meet the SMART criteria should do so for themselves and their own understanding of the lesson. An objective probably won't work as a purpose statement, as students are likely to get lost in the details. Students want to know what they are going to learn and how they will be expected to demonstrate their understanding.

Consider the following objective for a biology class designed to meet the SMART criteria:

> By the end of the period, students will describe the role of DNA in the creation of proteins by summarizing the process in writing.

This objective is useful for teachers. It has a time component and mentions specific content and a measurable outcome. But even though it meets the SMART criteria, we would argue that it is not very useful for students. First, while time limits are important in teaching, we're not convinced that they are necessary for a purpose statement. Second, when the purpose statement includes a task, students pay more attention to the task rather than to what they are expected to learn. For us, a better content purpose statement, based on the objective that the teacher has written, would read as follows:

> Explain the role of DNA in the creation of proteins.

In this case, students are immediately alerted to what they are expected to learn. They assume that the teacher will structure class time to ensure that they do, in fact, learn this and that they will be held accountable for doing so. Thus, the purpose statement is focusing for students, while not being so narrow as to limit their understanding.

Standards Versus Purpose Statements

As states increased the development of content standards in the 1980s, the standards effectively replaced the objectives that teachers posted for their students. (We even worked for a superintendent once who required standards to be posted on classroom walls and principals to check for them during their classroom observations.) However, replacing objectives with standards was actually a step backward in education. Although we believe that objectives may be overkill for students, at least they focus on what students are learning at the moment. Imagine the classroom that has the following 6th grade standard posted on the wall:

> Explain the significance of Greek mythology to the everyday life of people in the region and how Greek literature continues to permeate our literature and language today, drawing from Greek mythology and epics, such as Homer's *Iliad* and *Odyssey*, and from *Aesop's Fables*. (California Department of Education, 2000, p. 25)

The first problem with this statement is that the content described is taught and learned over several days, if not weeks. Our experience suggests that a purpose statement should focus on what can be accomplished today, rather than over several days. As it stands, this standard posing as a purpose statement is likely to be seen as wallpaper by students because it will be posted for so long. Second, there are too many ideas wrapped up in the statement. What should the students focus on? What, specifically, are they supposed to learn, and why?

Standards are meant to be unpacked and unwrapped, not simply posted on the wall (Ainsworth, 2003; Jackson, 2009). All kinds of excellent processes have been developed, such as Understanding by Design (Wiggins & McTighe, 2005), to ensure both that teacher lessons are based on standards and that students know what is expected of them. Many states are now adopting the Common Core State Standards, which will provide a new opportunity for teachers to focus on content and what they want students to learn. Again, simply posting one of the common core standards will not focus students on what they need to learn now.

Purpose and Inquiry

Some educators believe that establishing a clear purpose is actually detrimental to inquiry-based lessons. In fact, we were recently talking with a science teacher who said, "I don't state the purpose because then the inquiry process is ruined and my students won't want to do the lab." We are puzzled by this attitude, especially given that the scientific process clearly suggests that researchers have a purpose for their investigations. Consider the steps of the scientific process:

1. Ask a question.
2. Do background research.
3. Construct a hypothesis.
4. Test your hypothesis by doing an experiment.
5. Analyze your data and draw a conclusion.
6. Communicate your results.

There is a purpose to each of these steps, and if the purpose is not identified, novices are likely to be confused and misinformed.

The science teacher with whom we spoke may have meant that purpose statements for inquiry-based lessons should be focused on *content* rather than *process*, as in the following example:

Identify outliers in data sets.

This statement provides students with information about what they should learn as they determine the validity of given data points. In this case, students are learning how to review their data sets before analyzing data to determine if any of the data points were entered incorrectly. Over time, they will learn about outliers and why some researchers remove them. Understanding the role of outliers is part of the inquiry and research process and one that most students need to be taught.

Or perhaps the science teacher meant that the purpose should be established at the outset of a lesson. One of the most common misconceptions about establishing purpose is that it has to be done as soon as students enter the room. This is simply not true. We believe that students need to understand the purpose of the lesson at some point during the course of it, but not necessarily at the very beginning. For example, when we read informational texts to our students, we don't always establish the purpose in advance of the reading. Often, we read parts of the text, invite students to talk with group members, draw connections between the text and their experiences, and then debate the information presented before revealing the purpose behind what we're doing. One of our colleagues, a physics teacher, rarely reveals the purpose in advance of a lab because she wants students to first have experiences that will then make the purpose statement relevant. In many cases, students hypothesize the purpose, asking their physics teacher about it, as they complete the lab.

Purpose and Attention

What *is* important from the outset is student attention. When the lesson begins with something that grabs students, the purpose does not have to be set in advance; at other times, the purpose can serve to focus students and gain their attention. There is a reciprocal relationship between purpose and attention, and one that is worthy of the teacher's time.

It has been said that teachers are really brainworkers, and thus should be knowledgeable about how the brain works so that we can more skillfully influence its development (Battro, Fischer, & Léna, 2008). The explosion of knowledge about the brain in recent years has led to an intersection of fields that share a common interest in its structure and function. Psychologists, neuroscientists, and educators have all come to appreciate how each specialty can inform the other, and have even dubbed this emerging field *neuroeducation* (Battro, Fischer, & Léna, 2008).

A major area of shared research among the disciplines is on the role of attention in learning. Attention is, after all, a psychological state of being that is evoked by the environment itself. The ability to pay attention for longer periods has both a developmental component (young children have a shorter span of attention than older ones) and a contextual one (we can sustain our attention when the object is of interest). However, what is often overlooked is that expertise also plays a role. A novice is

not especially good at attending to the most salient information in the environment; to someone who isn't quite sure what
to pay attention to, everything and nothing seem important
all at once. You've seen this happen whenever you're in the
company of someone who possesses a high degree of expertise.
Perhaps you're in a museum with your friend the art buff, and
she points out the unique brushstrokes that are characteristic of
a particular painter. To you, the painting may simply be a pleas-
ing image, but to your expert friend it's replete with telltale
details. In the same way, a novice learner of multiplication may
overlook a pattern that emerges, or fail to see that an operation
is really rapid addition. A well-crafted purpose by the classroom
expert helps the novice attend to these nuances.

Your art-loving friend didn't simply pay attention; she knew
what to look for and how to look for it. Her brain functions
as a network of operations that are not well understood. Her
attention influences and is influenced by perception, memory,
and learning. In the same way, you learned something that you
didn't know before because she took the time to point it out
to you. As you listened to her, you focused your attention to
screen out the voices of other patrons (selective attention),
shifted it rapidly back and forth between what she was saying and the painting itself (alternating attention), and com-
manded yourself not to allow your mind to wander (sustained
attention). She paused to make sure you were following what
she was saying and checked your understanding by engaging
you in conversation. It's the same way in the classroom: Attention is jointly constructed, and each person plays a part.

The real trick is whether you remember what your friend said
after you leave the museum. Again, attention plays a key role.
Your friend can help you remember information if she tells you

how it relates to something you already know. For instance, she may tell you that the visible brushstrokes in a painting were a feature of the Impressionist painters. You immediately recall what you know about this period from an art history class you took in college. You may even think to yourself, "Hmm, that's interesting," and consciously decide to remember it. Both of you are building your schema about Impressionism, and your interaction reinforces your existing knowledge in the process of adding new knowledge. Establishing purpose not only focuses the learner's attention on the information to be learned, but also reinforces what has been previously learned.

Perhaps you can appreciate why the fields of psychology, education, and neuroscience find themselves drawn together. Understanding how the brain works involves psychological, cognitive, and biological perspectives; none stands completely apart from the others. Our field's expertise is in the cognitive/behavioral realm. Like the friend in the art museum, we can interpret what we observe for our science colleagues. And one of the most influential theories of cognition is the gradual release of responsibility.

Purpose and Gradual Release of Responsibility

The gradual release of responsibility model has its roots in the work of Campione (1981) and colleagues, who developed what they came to call a "cognitive apprenticeship model." They describe the role of the teacher across six phases: "(1) models expert behavior; (2) monitors the group's understanding; (3) engages in on-line diagnosis of emerging competence; (4) pushes for deeper understanding; (5) scaffolds the weaker students' emerging competence; and (6) fades into the background whenever the students are able to take charge of their own learning" (Brown & Campione, 1996, p. 122). The development of this model was intended to strike a middle ground between purely discovery learning and a strictly teacher-led model of telling, rather than teaching. Pearson and Gallagher (1983) applied this approach to the development of reading comprehension, describing a framework that included shared, guided, and independent reading. Calling the framework "gradual release of responsibility," they emphasized the reciprocal relationship between the cognitive burdens of the student and teacher: As the student gains expertise, the cognitive responsibility shifts to him or her, and the teacher takes on a more supportive (rather than directive) role.

We have built on the work of these researchers to articulate an instructional framework that builds the cognitive and metacognitive skills of learners. Drawing particularly from the work of Vygotsky (1978) in the realm of the social nature of learning, we have illustrated our framework as a series of teaching phases that together serve to build knowledge and deepen understanding (see Figure 1.1). These phases—the focus lesson, guided instruction, collaborative learning, and independent learning—are all influenced by the established purpose. (An overview of this model is presented in our book, *Better Learning through Structured Teaching* [2008].) Importantly, these phases occur in a different order depending on the purpose of the lesson.

Purpose and the Focus Lesson

Purpose is established in the focus lesson, when the teacher introduces and demonstrates concepts or skills that are new to students. When kindergarten teacher Mitzi Levinson says, "Today we're going to learn about the differences between

Figure 1.1
Gradual Release of Responsibility

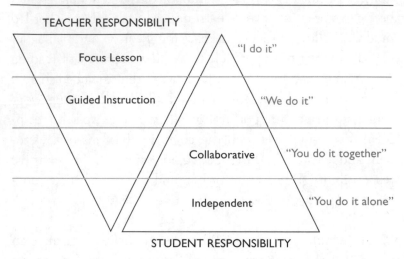

Source: From *Better Learning Through Structured Teaching* (p. 4), by D. Fisher and N. Frey, 2008, Alexandria, VA: ASCD. Copyright 2008 by ASCD.

triangles and squares, and we'll work together to sort them," she is establishing purpose for her students. "You'll be explaining how you decide what kind of shape you have." She models her thinking about the shapes as she chooses one and holds it up: "Now I'm looking at this one, and I am thinking about what I know about shapes," she offers. "The first thing I'll do is count the sides: one, two, three sides. There's only one shape I know of that's got three sides, and that's a triangle. I'm going to match it to the shape on the box to be sure," she says, holding it up to a labeled triangle on the sorting box. "Yes, it matches, so I know I should put it in here."

By initially establishing the purpose, Ms. Levinson draws her students' attention to the concepts that she wants them to learn and further explains how they will explore the concepts today. As she thinks aloud, she shares her decision-making process. While further experiences with the shapes will be needed, the focus lesson lays the groundwork.

Because the focus lesson is brief (only 5 to 15 minutes), Ms. Levinson knows that she needs to find out what her students have absorbed. This occurs during guided instruction.

Purpose and Guided Instruction

The guided instruction phase provides the teacher with information about how well students absorbed the initial instruction, as well as any misconceptions or partial understandings that the students may have. The teacher checks for understanding, asks questions to activate background knowledge or reflective thinking, and offers cues as needed to shift attention more overtly to sources of information. When these scaffolds fail, the teacher temporarily reassumes cognitive responsibility to provide direct explanation and modeling.

Purpose is essential to this phase of learning, as the teacher needs to have a clear vision for what exactly to assess. A lack of purpose can devolve into low-level measurement of compliance and assignment completion, rather than learning. If Ms. Levinson did not have a learning purpose in mind, her assessment of the students would be a strict tally of correct or incorrect outward behaviors. Fortunately, because her purpose is clear, the scaffolds that she can offer Joseph, a student having difficulty, are more helpful. As she sits with the boy while he sorts the shapes, she analyzes his errors and asks, "Joseph, can you tell me what you know about triangles and squares?" When Joseph correctly explains that the two shapes have a different number of sides, Ms. Levinson says, "Show me how you decide if the shape is a triangle or a square." As Joseph counts the sides, Ms. Levinson notices that he doesn't have a reliable technique for counting, and often counts the same side twice as he turns the shape. "As I'm watching you, I think I can see where you're making the mistake," she says. "Let me show you a different way." She places a shape on the desk and tells Joseph she is not going to move it, then places one finger on the side from which she begins. "When I get back to the place I started, I stop. Now you try it." In this case, Ms. Levinson's established purpose helps her recognize that the student understands the concept, but lacks a reliable technique.

Purpose and Collaborative Learning

Consistent with Vygotsky's tenet that all learning is social, we believe strongly in the power of collaborative learning to consolidate understanding and refine skills. As students move forward in their growing mastery of a topic, they need time with fellow learners to clarify and consolidate their knowledge. In some cases, such collaboration also exposes what they don't yet know. The opportunity to make mistakes and have the time and support to correct them can lead to a more solid understanding—a concept known as productive failure (Kapur, 2008).

Purpose plays a role in peer learning in that students have an expectation of what they are supposed to do. Let's return to Ms. Levinson's class. She sets the purpose again, explaining that students will work in small groups to sort large versions of the shapes: "Remember, this is a time when you get a chance to tell each other why you know a shape is a triangle or a square." As the students place the shapes into large plastic buckets, they use a language frame to extend their academic language in mathematics. Each table has a chart that says, "I know it is a _____ because _____." Ms. Levinson sits with each small group, providing guided instruction when the students are not able to resolve problems on their own.

Purpose and Independent Learning

As students move toward mastery, they assume more cognitive responsibility for their learning. In-class independent learning happens most commonly through reading and writing tasks; out-of-class independent learning is usually called homework. We believe debate around the usefulness of homework overlooks a glaring problem—namely, traditional homework occurs too early in the instructional cycle. Consider the purpose that Ms. Levinson sets for her kindergarten students: learning the differences between triangles and squares. This isn't a concept that is completely mastered in one lesson. Students need many experiences with the shapes to solidify their understanding. Ms. Levinson extends what they have been learning together by using an out-of-class task that they are reaching mastery on. She tells her students, "When you go home tonight, I'd like for you to find something in your house that is similar to a triangle or square. Choose one of the paper shapes to help you find a shape that looks like it. You can draw a picture or write the name of the object you find on your shape. Tomorrow you'll each tell us about the shapes you found and we'll sort them."

Ms. Levinson has in-class independent learning for her students to do as well. After choosing a paper shape, they are to look around the classroom to find an object that is similar. Joseph chooses a picture book that looks like his square, while Corrine selects a triangular wooden building block. Ms.

Levinson talks briefly with each student to determine what he or she knows about the shape. Tomorrow they'll continue, now talking about objects that are more abstract.

Indicators of Success

Figure 1.2 contains a rubric that can be used to identify areas of strength and need in terms of establishing purpose. As a note of caution, using a rubric such as this one to evaluate teacher performance is probably not very helpful and could result in hurt feelings and conflict. Instead, we suggest that the rubric be used as a needs assessment following a conversation about quality. When teachers, coaches, and administrators agree on quality, amazing conversations can be held. Without agreements about quality, even agreements that grow and develop over time, conversations can become defensive and accusatory. We strongly suggest taking the time to talk about quality and to reach agreements about quality before providing one another with feedback.

We believe that all of the indicators on this rubric are important considerations, and have developed descriptors for each of them. We'd like to say that we consistently teach at the "4" level, but that would not be true; although we aim for a 4 each time we teach, we don't always reach our goal. The rubric helps us to reflect on our teaching and to identify areas of strength and need. For example, Nancy knows that she is very strong in the area of linking lessons to a larger theme, problem, project, or question. When colleagues need help in this area, they often seek her out for assistance. Doug is strong at developing content and language components for each lesson. He likes to think about the linguistic demands of the lesson and how to help students master content. As such, he is often asked about the linguistic demands of a lesson and how to develop the language component of the purpose statement.

Conclusion

All of the indicators on the rubric in Figure 1.2 are further described and defined in the chapters that follow. They are presented in the same order as in the rubric, but that's not to say that you have to read them in any particular order. If you need, for example, immediate information about meaningful experiences that are linked to purpose, skip to Chapter 6 and find out more. If you want to know why we think it is critical that students can explain the purpose in their own words and why the purpose should have relevance for students, jump to Chapters 3 and 4. We do hope that you'll eventually read the whole book, as it contains our best thinking about this very important aspect of teaching and learning—establishing purpose. As author W. Clement Stone said, "Definiteness of purpose is the starting point of all achievement."

Figure 1.2

Indicators of Success—Establishing Purpose

Indicators	Phase 4—Exemplary	Phase 3—Proficient	Phase 2—Approaching	Phase 1—Minimal
The established purpose focuses on student learning, rather than an activity, assignment, or task.	The established purpose requires students to use critical and creative thinking to acquire information, resolve a problem, apply a skill, or evaluate a process. The lesson's work is clearly linked to a theme, problem, project, or question the class is investigating.	The established purpose is linked to a theme, problem, project, or question, but the lesson's work is primarily on an isolated activity, assignment, or task, rather than an enduring understanding.	The established purpose mostly contains statements about activities, assignments, or tasks, with minimal linkage to a theme, problem, project, or question. The work is primarily reproductive in nature.	The established purpose fails to link the lesson's classroom work to any theme, problem, project, or question. Instead, an agenda of isolated activities, assignments, or tasks is listed.
The established purpose contains both content and language components.	The established purpose contains statements about grade- or course-appropriate content as well as language demands that can be learned and accomplished today.	The established purpose contains content and language demand components that are grade- or course-appropriate, but are too broad and require several lessons to learn.	The established purpose omits either the content or language component. It is grade- or content-appropriate, but is too broad and requires several lessons to accomplish.	The statement is not grade- or course-appropriate. The statement is vague and does not provide students with a clear sense of what is expected and what is to be learned.
Students understand the relevance of the established purpose.	Randomly selected students can explain the stated purposes of the lesson and how they are linked to a theme, problem, project, or question. The student recognizes the relevance of the purpose beyond the classroom or for learning's sake as well as how information can be found, used, created, or shared.	Randomly selected students can restate the purpose and report how the purpose is related to a theme, problem, project, or question. The students may recognize some relevance to their own life or technology.	Randomly selected students can restate the relevance established by the teacher, but do not see connections with a theme, problem, project, or question. They are tentative or unsure of the usefulness of the learning beyond the classroom.	The statements of randomly selected students emphasize compliance, rather than a link to a theme, problem, project, or question. They are not able to link their learning to usefulness beyond the classroom.

Indicators	Phase 4—Exemplary	Phase 3—Proficient	Phase 2—Approaching	Phase 1—Minimal
Students can explain the established purpose in their own words.	Randomly selected students can explain or demonstrate what they are learning in their own words and what is expected of them for the lesson.	Randomly selected students can accurately restate the purpose of the lesson using their teacher's words.	Randomly selected students can restate portions of the purpose of the lesson. These partial explanations reflect the teacher's wording more than their own.	Randomly selected students are unable to correctly state the purpose of the lesson.
The teacher designs meaningful experiences and outcomes aligned with the established purpose.	The established purpose requires students to actively construct meaning through interaction with the teacher, the content materials, and each other. Students receive feedback about the task, the processing of the task, self-regulation, and about the self as person.	The established purpose requires interaction with the teacher, content materials, and each other, but the teacher, rather than the students, mostly develops the meaning. The feedback students receive focuses mainly on the task with some information about the process used.	The established purpose requires some interaction, but is mostly confined to reproduction and recall of content. Students may not see the task as meaningful and receive feedback that is not specific and only focused on the task.	The established purpose focuses on a one-way transmission model of instruction, with little or no interaction with teacher, content, or each. Students receive little timely and specific feedback other than whether or not they completed the task correctly.
The teacher has a plan for determining when the established purpose has been met.	The teacher can explain a system to check for understanding during and after the lesson and how this information is used to inform instructional decisions within the current lesson and the lessons that follow. The format of the lesson is designed to allow the teacher to respond to students' misconceptions or partial understandings.	The teacher can explain how he or she checks for understanding during and after the lesson. The results of the lesson's work are used to make instructional decisions about the next lesson.	The teacher checks for understanding at the end of the lesson only. He or she can explain how these results are used to make instructional decisions about the next lesson.	The tasks are graded, but do not drive instruction. Instead, the emphasis is on task completion, rather than on gauging student learning to design the next lesson.

2

Focusing on Learning Targets, Not Tasks

Good purpose setting is analogous to putting on a live theater production. Before the curtain rises, planning and rehearsals take place. From the audience's perspective, what occurred prior to the performance is of little consequence. But the actors, musicians, and stagehands know that the quality of the performance is dependent on what occurred during the weeks that led up to this moment. Likewise, development of an effective purpose is the final result of lots of behind-the-scenes planning.

The Play's the Thing

As we noted in the previous chapter, it's important to refrain from establishing a purpose so specific and detailed that the learner loses sight of the big picture. Much as a play is more than just a series of scenes, so too is your teaching. Too often, students are not able to see how what they learned on Tuesday relates to what they're learning on Friday. A well-established purpose makes these connections, while further making the day's learning meaningful, relevant, and interesting.

Activities, assignments, and tasks are meant to move students forward from gaining initial knowledge to applying it. This progression isn't always readily apparent to novice teachers. We both remember approaching our student-teaching assignments as fixed periods that needed to be filled with activities. It didn't take long for us to realize (with the help of our mentors) that there was more to teaching than just keeping students occupied. In the same way, we don't want students to regard their education as an endless series of assignments that must be completed. In fact, whenever a student of ours says, "Do we need to know this for the test?" it's a reminder that, at least for that student, we didn't do a good job of setting the purpose.

A purpose statement can't stand on an assignment alone. "The purpose today is to do the odd-numbered problems on page 98" is, frankly, a lousy statement. "The purpose today is to learn about lowest common denominators and how to use them to solve problems, and you'll use the odd-numbered problems on page 98 to practice them with your team" is better. The first statement leaves the student to conclude that page 98 is busy work; the second statement encourages the student to see that page 98 is a resource for practicing problem-solving. There's a fair amount of criticism from some quarters that textbooks are used inappropriately, and we would agree. If the purpose is nothing more than slogging through page after page, then it's reflective of poor teaching. The problem has less to do with the textbook itself than with the inadequate way it is being used. "Read Chapter 4 and answer the questions at the end" is do-it-yourself school, not teaching and learning. A well-crafted purpose statement makes sure to address why and how activities, tasks, and assignments move the learning agenda foreward.

Establishing purpose is essential for developing the metacognitive awareness necessary for creative and critical thinking. A purpose statement that focuses only on the *assignment* limits students' ability to think about their own learning; one that focuses on *learning* provides students with an opportunity to reflect on their newfound knowledge. Teachers who establish the latter type of purpose statement can return to it once their students are done with their assigned work, asking students about what they learned and what they're having difficulty with. In this way, the purpose statement becomes the touchstone for encouraging reflection and deepening levels of understanding.

Over time, and with practice, students who reflect on the purpose of their learning develop critical and creative thinking skills, which are the hallmark of an educated citizen. The Common Core Standards were developed in an effort to prepare college- and career-ready students who are "fully prepared for the future" (National Governor's Association, 2010). We want students who can use (and not simply parrot) what they have learned. To do so, students need lots of opportunities to think critically and creatively in the classroom. It is not enough to expect that students will somehow be able to do so after they leave high school. The fact is that very young children are capable of thinking critically and creatively, but may not have many opportunities to do so in classrooms where basic skills acquisition drives the curriculum (Costa, 2001).

Fennimore and Tinzmann (1990) identified characteristics of a curriculum that promotes critical and creative thinking:

- The scope promotes in-depth learning.
- Content and process are integrated and situated in authentic tasks.
- The tasks are sequenced to reflect increasing cognitive and metacognitive challenge.
- The curriculum fosters connections to the learner's background knowledge and prior experiences.

Students use their creative and critical processes as they acquire information, apply skills, resolve problems, and evaluate processes. Each of these actions represents a growing understanding of the content and processes associated with what the students are learning. We're a bit leery of the terms "higher order" and "lower order" thinking skills, because they seem to falsely suggest that some thinking skills are more valuable than others. The fact is that each type of thinking represents a dimension of understanding, and is predicated on the notion that you need to know the "what" of something in order to appreciate the "why."

Establishing purpose that helps develop critical and creative thinking in students requires the kind of backward planning that Wiggins and McTighe discuss in their book *Understanding by Design* (2005). They advise beginning by identifying understandings that are "enduring, at the heart of the discipline, needing uncoverage, [and] potentially engaging" (p. 23). These enduring understandings should invite a view from six different vantage points: explanation, interpretation, application, perspective taking, empathy, and self-knowledge. Educators should match these six facets of understanding to the means for assessing student understanding and mastery, and then develop organizing questions that require learning of the subject in order to be answered. Only then can a sequence of lessons be designed that will lead students to the identified learning targets.

We have developed a diagram that illustrates the necessary elements for planning purpose statements "behind the scenes" (see Figure 2.1). These factors converge to create effective statements that drive instruction, learning, and assessment. The planning process begins with the development of curriculum that is organized around standards-based themes, problems, projects, or questions that promote creative and critical thinking.

Developing a Standards-based Theme, Project, Problem, or Question

Grade-level or content standards have long been used as the first point of reference for developing units of instruction. Since the advent of content standards in the early 1990s, these documents have outlined the cognitive boundaries of courses. Many districts and schools have developed units of study based on close analysis of these standards, and they can serve as an excellent resource for organizing curriculum and planning instruction. With the rapid adoption of the Common Core Standards, it is likely that we will see a resurgence of this kind of work. One expected benefit is that units of instruction and accompanying curricular materials will be developed more rapidly, through widespread sharing of ideas and resources.

Many teachers organize their curriculum using the content as an anchor. The rationale behind this process is to unify information in such a way as to build schema and foreground the relationships between topics and disciplines. Middle and high schools often pursue interdisciplinary units—for example, an

Figure 2.1

A Planning Process for Establishing Purpose

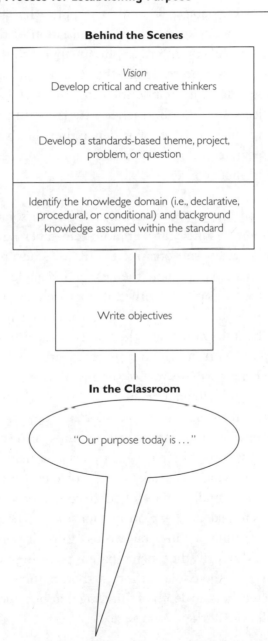

English teacher might team up with a World History teacher to develop a unit on the literature and history of the Holocaust. Such a unit encourages students to apply what they know about the events of an era to an examination of the literary expressions of the era. Interdisciplinary approaches are popular with teachers, who recognize that the background knowledge necessary for deeper understanding can be co-constructed across subjects. In addition, teachers often report that they can spend more time on issues that demand evaluative and creative perspectives in interdisciplinary units because students simply learn more content.

Theme-based instruction remains a feature in some elementary classrooms. Nancy can certainly remember her first year of teaching, when she organized units of study for her 1st grade students around simple themes such as apples. However, she soon grew dissatisfied with this approach, as she realized that the students weren't actually learning that much about apples. (She also wasn't sure they *needed* to learn that much about apples.) Fortunately, her more experienced colleagues introduced her to more robust themes that were worthy of attention. Before long, her students were organizing their thinking around themes such as explorers. They examined the lives of people such as astronaut Mae Jemison in science and Leif Erickson in social studies. They became math explorers themselves, delving into tricky word problems using algebraic thinking. They studied maps of their community to identify good places to take dogs exploring. Her students became word explorers, gleefully adding "big words" to their personal dictionaries. Although the theme-based planning was pretty straightforward, the choice of robust themes showed an inexperienced teacher the depth of thinking that her students were capable of, even at their young age.

Problems and projects can also serve as a catalyst for unit planning. Again, the first consideration is whether the projects are rich enough to warrant the instructional investment. A unit designed primarily to move a project to completion is not going to offer much in the way of learning. For instance, a unit that is based on writing a research paper offers little room for learning beyond the successful completion of the assignment. However, a research paper that is a major outcome of, say, a chemistry unit on finding out how elements are added to the Periodic Table *is* meaningful. Possible topics for such a paper could include finding out information about the latest element added to the table (i.e., who discovered it and why), exploring the debate about the naming of elements, or considering the projected effects of the Hadron particle accelerator on newly discovered elements. Through the lens of such topics, the research paper becomes a necessary step but not the main reason for learning about the Periodic Table.

At the high school where we work, schoolwide essential questions are used to encourage inquiry and cross-disciplinary partnerships. Nominations are collected each spring from faculty and students, and the entire school votes on their favorites. The top four questions are used the following school year. Here are the essential questions chosen for a recent school year:

- What is beauty and/or beautiful?
- Does gender matter?
- Who are your heroes and role models?
- What's worth fighting, and even dying, for?

During the first quarter, 12th grade English students read books such as *The Birthmark* by Nathaniel Hawthorne, 9th grade students explored the golden ratio in algebra, and 10th graders examined symmetrical and asymmetrical development of organisms in biology. Importantly, the content is dictated by the standards for the course, not the essential questions. However, these questions allow teachers to organize their curriculum in different ways, promote interdisciplinary planning, and most important, provide a higher degree of relevance as students deepen their knowledge across the six facets of understanding (Wiggins & McTighe, 2005).

Identifying Knowledge Domain and Background Knowledge Assumed Within the Standard

By the time you've reached this step of the planning process, you're well on your way to establishing a clear purpose. You have consulted the standards for the grade level or content to determine the breadth and depth of learning expected of your students. You know what you want your students to know and be able to do, and you've begun the backward-planning process to determine what students will learn each day. You'll base the daily learning on a theme, project, problem, or question that organizes the standards into meaningful units of study. But simply posting the theme or question will not ensure that students learn at high levels. As teachers, we have to determine what our students already know as well as what they still need to learn. What they already know can be identified using background knowledge assessments. What they still need to learn can be categorized in three ways: declarative, procedural, or conditional knowledge (Paris, Lipson, & Wixson, 1983).

Assessing Background Knowledge

To assess background knowledge, the teacher has to determine what core background knowledge (as opposed to incidental knowledge) is necessary for students to understand the new information to be learned. It is useful to have the specific standards you'll be teaching available for cross-reference as you work through the following questions to distinguish between core background knowledge and incidental knowledge:

1. *Representation:* Is the information foundational or essential to understanding the main concept (core), or interesting but peripheral (incidental)?
2. *Transmission:* Does the information require multiple exposures and experiences (core), or can it be easily explained or defined using a label, fact, or detail (incidental)?
3. *Transferability:* Will the information be required to understand future concepts (core), or is it specific to one topic and not likely to be used in the near future (incidental)?
4. *Endurance:* Will the information be remembered after the details are forgotten (core), or will it likely not be recalled (incidental)?

As the above questions indicate, all background knowledge is not equally relevant. Consider, for example, a student who shares an experience from a middle school science project on electrical circuits, talking on and on about how they work, when he finds out his class will be reading *The Circuit*—a book about a migrant family of farm workers. The student may have extensive background knowledge, but it isn't relevant to the content to be studied.

Following are a few relatively easy ways to assess background knowledge and provide examples of each assessment tool using as an example a unit of study on the Roman Empire.

Cloze Assessment. Cloze is a tool used to assess comprehension or readability in which a reading selection is provided with certain words deleted (Taylor, 1953). The student provides closure by inserting the appropriate words according to context clues. This informal, criterion-referenced assessment is useful for teachers for several reasons. First, it is flexible enough to allow teachers to assess large groups of students at the same time or to assess students individually. Second, the information gathered through the assessment can be used to select reading material for students that is challenging, but not frustrating. And third, it allows the teacher to determine which students have sufficient background knowledge to understand the text. The steps of a cloze assessment to determine whether the text is at the students' reading level are as follows:

1. Select a passage of approximately 250–300 words from one of the readings that students will complete as part of a unit.
2. If the passage ends in the middle of a sentence, include the entire sentence to be sure that the break in syntax is not confusing to the reader.
3. After the first 25 or so words in the passage, delete every fifth word and insert a straight line in its place.
4. The passage should contain approximately 50 straight lines after deletions have been made.
5. Without setting a time limit, ask students to insert the missing words.
6. Each correct closure is worth two points, with no deductions for misspellings.
7. The assessment is scored as follows: 58–100 points indicates an *independent* reading level, 44–57 points indicates an *instructional* reading level, and fewer than 44 points indicates a *frustrational* reading level.

Once the results are tallied, you will have a general idea of the type of text to use when beginning instruction. And by studying the types of errors that students make, you can analyze the student's ability to comprehend the passage. While many educators may suggest that the exact word must be inserted, we believe that the inserted word should be counted as correct if it is the appropriate part of speech and does not alter the meaning of the text. The student's performance, rather than the score, is the key to this successful integration of assessment and instruction.

In terms of background knowledge, the cloze procedure provides teachers with an idea about the type of words that come to mind for the student. Of course, there is significant variation in word understanding, but if the student can supply an appropriate word for the passage, it is likely that student has the relevant background knowledge.

Figure 2.2 contains an example of a cloze passage for a reading related to the Roman Empire. On the student version, the underlined words would be eliminated, but we left them in to demonstrate the correct passage and how easy it is to create this type of assessment.

Caption Writing. Asking students to write captions or descriptions of illustrations or photos can provide you with a reasonable understanding of their relevant background knowledge. If students can supply appropriate vocabulary for the images they're seeing, they probably have already learned related concepts. For example, in the unit on the Roman Empire, the teacher might project a picture of the Parthenon on the wall, along with two or three other images related to the empire, then give students about 10 minutes to describe what they see.

Figure 2.2
Cloze Assessment Passage Example

People lived in Italy long before the rise of the Roman Empire. According to legend, Rome <u>was</u> established by twin brothers <u>named</u> Romulus and Remus, who <u>were</u> raised by wolves. People <u>from</u> other regions began settling <u>and</u> trading around 750 BCE, <u>including</u> Etruscans from northern Italy <u>and</u> Greek traders. The Etruscans <u>turned</u> Rome from a village <u>to</u> a city by building <u>roads</u> and temples. They were <u>cruel</u> and were overthrown. The <u>people</u> of Rome established a <u>republic</u>.

The Greek traders shared <u>their</u> art, culture, and ideas <u>with</u> Romans. The Greeks were <u>famous</u> for their beautiful architecture <u>and</u> art, and the Romans <u>admired</u> it. They also worshiped <u>many</u> gods and goddesses. They <u>told</u> elaborate stories of their <u>gods'</u> adventures. We call these <u>stories</u> myths.

People in the <u>ancient</u> world lived short and <u>harsh</u> lives. The work was <u>hard</u> and disease claimed many. <u>People</u> began their adult lives <u>when</u> they were still teenagers. <u>As</u> with other societies, women <u>and</u> the poor had few <u>rights</u>. Many societies needed enslaved <u>people</u> captured from wars to <u>do</u> the work and building.

Here's an example of what a student might write:

> I know this one because I've been to Greece. I can't remember what it's called, but it was a temple for Athena. She was kinda like a Greek Goddess. It was also a place where they buried people, and there were celebrations there. It has a lot of different buildings that are mostly falling down now.

Reading this student's passage, the teacher will note the background knowledge and be able to refer to it throughout the lesson.

Word Sorts. Another way to determine what students already know is to ask them to sort words. Sorts can either be closed (in which the teacher furnishes categories) or open (in which students develop their own categories). Again, this task requires that students draw on their word knowledge, which is the representation of their background knowledge. A quick analysis of the ways in which students sort words can inform the teacher of what the student does and does not yet understand.

Figure 2.3 contains a sample word sort for the Roman Empire unit. When Heather put "democracy" under the category "All Societies," her teacher had a clue about needed instruction. Similarly, when Brianna put "polis" under the category "Persia," her teacher hypothesized that she didn't understand the ideas. And when Onisha put "Pharaoh" under the category "Egypt," her teacher knew that she had some understanding of the Egyptian civilization.

Figure 2.3
Word Sort Example

Note: This can be a whiteboard, blackboard, or handout activity. Students will sort the words according to the following four categories: *Greece, Egypt, Persia,* and *All Societies.*

Agora	exports	polis	wealth
democracy	Mediterranean	Acropolis	Cyrus
architecture	enslaved people	King	Pharaoh
wars	rich and poor people		

Opinionnaires. Opinionnaires are tools for eliciting attitudes about a topic. Understanding students' attitudes is important in assessing their background knowledge, and opinionnaires are designed to "help students to broaden their repertoire of interpretive strategies by encouraging them to consider and evaluate authors' and characters' uses of important themes and ideas and by helping them to connect literature and life" (White & Johnson, 2001, p. 120). Opinionnaires can take a variety of formats, but all feature a series of statements that are meant to be provocative or controversial. Most opinionnaires do not allow for a neutral response, but rather ask the respondent whether he or she agrees with a statement. We like to also provide space for students to provide a reason for their opinion. An example of this format related to the Roman Empire appears in Figure 2.4. Analyzing the responses on opinionnaires reveals the extent of students' background knowledge.

Figure 2.4

Opinionnaire Example

BEFORE		AFTER
I 2 3 4 Why?	The Roman Civilization was the greatest of the ancient world.	I 2 3 4 Why?
I 2 3 4 Why?	It was difficult to be a poor person in the ancient world.	I 2 3 4 Why?
I 2 3 4 Why?	It was difficult to be a woman in the ancient world.	I 2 3 4 Why?
I 2 3 4 Why?	If it hadn't been for the Greeks, the Roman civilization would not have risen to such power.	I 2 3 4 Why?

I = Strongly disagree
2 = Disagree
3 = Agree
4 = Strongly agree

Determining Knowledge Domain

In addition to identifying what students already know, teachers have to understand the type of knowledge that students still need to gain. As we noted previously, there are at least three types of knowledge: declarative, procedural, and conditional. In explaining each of these types of knowledge, we'll use our personal trainer as an example. (Yes, we finally gave in and hired someone to help us stay fit.)

Declarative knowledge is the "what" of learning—that is, the content. Our trainer has a great deal of declarative knowledge—he knows how different muscles work, what the signs of fatigue are, what different fitness contraptions do, and so on. Procedural knowledge is the "how" of learning—knowledge of the rules, processes, or procedures necessary to accomplish a task. Our trainer understands the rules for safely lifting weights and how to plan a workout that has, as she says, a balance of push and pull exercises. Conditional knowledge is the "when," "where," and "why" of learning—in other words, it concerns the contexts and circumstances in which specific knowledge should be applied. Our trainer knows that the same workout will not be effective for both of us, and she uses her knowledge of our strengths, goals, and needs to plan the session. She often has to modify the training on the spot, as was the case when Doug showed up with minor back pain.

Importantly, our trainer would not be effective with knowledge in only one of the three domains. Knowing the names of muscles and how they work is important, and so is making modifications to an exercise routine. One type of knowledge is not better than another. Our job as teachers is to determine which domains of knowledge students need and to develop lessons that develop that knowledge.

Returning to the Roman Empire unit, the teacher might identify the following areas as important for his students to learn:

- *Declarative*—knowledge of the location of the empire
  and its geographical features, the different rights
  accorded to different people in the empire, religious
  differences among Roman citizens, the different
  groups that invaded the empire
- *Procedural*—knowledge of the timeline of the Roman
  Empire, whether conquests were necessary, why
  Brutus killed Caesar
- *Conditional*—knowledge of what made city-states
  work, the circumstances behind the fall of Rome, the
  role of the ruler in Rome versus that of rulers in the
  present day

Once students' background knowledge has been assessed and
the types of knowledge needed have been identified, you're
ready to consider the various objectives needed to ensure student learning. Remember that objectives can provide you with
guidance about the amount of time necessary for students to
master the content as well as how that mastery will be assessed.
The objectives aren't the purpose, but the purpose comes from
the objective. The objective can require days or weeks to
accomplish; the purpose is what students will learn today.

Writing Objectives

The most well-known system for writing objectives is Bloom's
Taxonomy (Bloom, 1956). Bloom's original taxonomy included
six categories: *knowledge, comprehension, application, analysis,
synthesis,* and *evaluation*. These are common knowledge for
most teachers, so we won't go into great detail here. For each
category, a number of different terms can be used to guide the
development of objectives. Figure 2.5 contains a list of terms
associated with each category of Bloom's taxonomy as well

Figure 2.5

Bloom's Taxonomy

Level	Key Words	Ms. Oxenhandler's Prompts
Knowledge Recall data or information.	defines, describes, identifies, knows, labels, lists, matches, names, outlines, recalls, recognizes, reproduces, selects, states	Where is … What did … Who was … When did … How many … Locate it in the story … Point to the …
Comprehension Understand the meaning, translation, interpolation, and interpretation of instructions and problems.	comprehends, converts, defends, distinguishes, estimates, explains, extends, generalizes, gives examples, infers, interprets, paraphrases, predicts, rewrites, summarizes, translates	Tell me in your own words … What does it mean … Give me an example of … Describe what … Illustrate the part of the story that … Make a map of … What is the main idea of …
Application Use a concept in a new situation or unprompted use of an abstraction.	applies, changes, computes, constructs, demonstrates, discovers, manipulates, modifies, operates, predicts, prepares, produces, relates, shows, solves, uses	What would happen to you if … Would you have done the same as … If you were there would you … How would you solve the problem … In the library, find information about …
Analysis Separate material or concepts into component parts so that its organizational structure may be understood.	analyzes, breaks down, compares, contrasts, diagrams, deconstructs, differentiates, discriminates, distinguishes, identifies, illustrates, infers, outlines, relates, selects, separates	What things would you have used … What other ways could … What things are similar/different? What part of this story was the most exciting? What things couldn't have happened in real life? What kind of person is … What caused _____ to act the way he/she did?

(continued)

Figure 2.5

Bloom's Taxonomy (continued)

Level	Key Words	Ms. Oxenhandler's Prompts
Synthesis Build a structure or pattern from diverse elements. Put parts together to form a whole, with emphasis on creating a new meaning or structure.	categorizes, combines, compiles, composes, creates, devises, designs, explains, generates, modifies, organizes, plans, rearranges, reconstructs, relates, reorganizes, revises, rewrites, summarizes, tells, writes	What would it be like if . . . What would it be like to live . . . Design a . . . Pretend you are a . . . What would have happened if . . . Why/why not? Use your imagination to draw a picture of . . . Add a new item on your own . . . Tell/write a different ending . . .
Evaluation Make judgments about the value of ideas or materials.	appraises, compares, concludes, contrasts, criticizes, critiques, defends, describes, discriminates, evaluates, explains, interprets, justifies, relates, summarizes, supports	Would you recommend this book? Why or why not? Select the best . . . Why is it the best? What do you think will happen to . . . Why do you think that? Could this story really have happened? Which character would you most like to meet? Was _____ good or bad? Why? Did you like the story? Why?

as prompts for their use, developed by our colleague Alicia Oxenhandler.

Bloom's Taxonomy was updated by Anderson and colleagues (2001) to reflect changes in instructional methods and 21st century skills. In the revised version, the six categories have been recast as *remembering, understanding, applying, analyzing, evaluating,* and *creating.* In addition to shifting the categories from nouns to verbs, the revised taxonomy places *creating* (i.e., *synthesis*) above *evaluating*. These terms are most often used to categorize the type of objectives for a lesson or unit.

Returning to the unit on the Roman Empire, the teacher might develop the following objectives:

- By the end of the second week of the six-week unit, the student will be able to identify the location of the Roman Empire and the geographical features of the empire as measured by a map test.
- By the third week of the unit, the student will create a visual timeline of the Roman Empire using computer software.
- By the fourth week of the unit, the student will defend his or her position regarding the use of conquests to maintain the Roman Empire in a class debate.
- By the fifth week of the unit, the student will describe the different rights accorded to different types of Roman citizens (men, women, Christians, slaves, etc.) in a first-person fictionalized account of daily life in the empire.
- By the end of the six-week unit, the student will defend Brutus for killing Caesar in a mock trial by discussing the roles of nationalism and personal freedom in the empire.
- By the end of the six-week unit, the student will produce an essay exploring a question related to the legacy of the Roman Empire (e.g., Why did city-states work? Why did Rome fall? Would Rome fall today? What was the role of the ruler in Rome, and how is this different today? Is the Roman Empire with us today?).

Each of the above objectives requires a series of instructional events designed to facilitate students' learning. The teacher will model his thinking about geography, read aloud from various sources (including the textbook), demonstrate how to debate, engage his students in productive group work for the mock trial, assign independent learning tasks (such as developing a timeline), and check students' understanding and reteach as necessary. Each of these events is guided by the teacher's understanding of one of the objectives; in other words, the objectives build students' knowledge, ensuring that students develop their understanding of the unit theme: "The Roman Empire: From Antiquity to Today."

As we have noted several times, objectives are helpful to the teacher, not the students. Less helpful still would be to simply post a standard on the wall and leave it there for six weeks. What the students need is a purpose for the work they're expected to do. Here are a few days' worth of possible content purpose statements that the teacher of the Roman Empire unit might develop for the first objective listed above ("By the end of the second week of the six-week unit, the student will be able to identify the location of the Roman Empire and the geographical features of the empire as measured by a map test"):

- Identify the location of Rome and the boundaries of the Roman Empire on a map.
- Name the land formations and geographical features in the Roman Empire circa CE 117.
- Understand the effect that at least three geographical features had on Roman civilization.
- Understand that the changing boundaries of the Roman Empire were based on conquests over time.

Each of these content purpose statements helps the teacher to stay focused and the students to know what is expected of them. Together, they build toward mastery of the objective and, eventually, the standard; separately, they clearly indicate that there is work to be done and there are things to learn, suggesting urgency and importance. It's the *purpose* that drives our daily work with students, alerts them to key ideas, and allows us to share our high expectations with them.

How Dare You Use "Understand"!

You might have noticed that two of the purpose statements included the word *understand*. Did you think this was a mistake? Or perhaps that the teacher was not up to par on his lesson planning? Or even that we were confused about what makes a good, SMART objective? When we first learned about writing objectives, we were told never to use the word *understand* because it's not measurable. In fact, Doug was told that he would not earn credit for any assignment in which *understand* was used for measuring student learning. We dutifully wrote lesson plan after lesson plan, careful to avoid the taboo word. Instead, we used words like *identify, describe, or explain*. We snickered when we saw our colleagues use the forbidden word. Then we realized something: The purpose statement can use the word *understand*, even if the objectives do not.

This realization was a huge relief for both of us, because students actually understand the word *understand*. They know that there will be a variety of different ways that their teachers ask them to demonstrate their understanding, often communicated through an outcome statement or learning task. Of course, that's not to say that *understand* is the only term you can use in a purpose statement; all kinds of verbs are useful. It's just that the word that we were prohibited from using when writing objectives is totally acceptable when communicating purpose.

Conclusion

At the beginning of this chapter, we used a theater analogy for the behind-the-scenes planning that occurs before the purpose statement debuts. This analogy should not be misconstrued as an endorsement of the "sage on the stage" model of teaching. There is a time for direct explanation, modeling, demonstrating, and thinking aloud—that time is during the focus lesson. However, for students to begin to assume cognitive responsibility, they need many opportunities to interact with the teacher, the content, and one another in collaborative and productive ways. These interactions are at the heart of effective purpose statements.

3

Including Both Content
and Language Components

In Chapter 2, we focused on learning targets and how to differentiate them from activities, assignments, and tasks. We also noted that themes, projects, problems, or questions have to be aligned with content or grade-level standards and expectations. In this chapter, we dig deeper into the process for determining purpose based on standards and what students need to know and be able to do. This chapter will help you develop objectives based on the type of knowledge—declarative, procedural, or conditional—that students need to demonstrate.

Identifying the purpose for any lesson requires an analysis of the standard being addressed, as well as an understanding of the linguistic demands of that standard. There really are two parts to every purpose statement: a content component and a language component. Sometimes, teachers address these in two separate statements; other times, teachers combine them as one. For example, an algebra teacher might state the purpose for a lesson this way:

> Using technical vocabulary, determine a second factor of
> a polynomial given a first factor.

Or, just as easily, this way:

> Today you will learn how to determine a second factor of a
> polynomial given a first factor. When you do so, I want you
> to use technical vocabulary, not the common or slang terms.

Either way works, provided that students understand the content they are learning as well as the language that they will use. It is clear in both of the above examples that the teacher wants her students to understand a specific skill, and she knows that using technical vocabulary is important in developing this understanding.

Unpacking Standards

To figure out the content component of a purpose statement, teachers have to unpack the standards. Our experience suggests that this is most easily done in grade-level or course-alike teams, so that ideas can be shared among teachers who all teach the same content. Working in a professional learning community to unpack the standards is rewarding on several levels (DuFour, DuFour, Eaker, & Karhanek, 2004). First, many hands make light work: When a team comes together to unpack standards, each teacher has less individual work to do. Second, the process results in vertical alignment across a grade or subject. We expect that students have had similar content in previous years so that there aren't gaps in their learning. Third, teachers share their instructional ideas with one another during these professional conversations. We should borrow ideas from our colleagues and try them out.

Of course, there are times when professional learning communities focused on unpacking standards don't work, and each individual teacher has to complete the process alone. It's tempting to buy a program that does this for you, but we caution against that tactic. Unpacking standards allows teachers to deeply understand the content standards such that the purpose statements and the resulting instruction are relevant and appropriate for students.

One of the ways that we have learned to unpack standards focuses on what students are expected to know and be able to do. We list a standard and then identify verbs (how students will demonstrate their understanding) and nouns (What students are required to know). As an example, let's use a 7th grade language arts standard from the Common Core State Standards (National Governors Association, 2010):

> Compare and contrast a written story, drama, or poem to its audio, filmed, staged, or multimedia version, analyzing the effects of techniques unique to each medium (e.g., lighting, sound, color, or camera focus and angles in a film).

In unpacking this standard, the verbs are *compare, contrast,* and *analyze.* Accordingly, students need to be taught how to compare and contrast as well as how to analyze. The standard is not asking students to argue that print is better or worse than other media, say, or to write a report about each medium; rather, students are expected to identify the similarities and differences between a printed text and a nonprint version of the same content. This is important: Comparing and contrasting requires students to identify *both* similarities and differences, not just the differences *or* similarities. In addition, the standard requires that students analyze specific techniques that are unique to each medium (e.g., how lighting influences their perception of a character in a film).

If we focus on the nouns in the standard, we see references to a number of text types (*written story*, *drama*, and *poem*) and media (*audio*, *filmed*, *staged*, and *multimedia* versions of text) as well as techniques (*lighting*, *sound*, *color*, *focus*, and *angles*). Students have to understand that the word *medium* in this context does not to refer to clothes size ("I wear a medium") or psychics ("She went to a medium to contact her ancestors"), but rather to the format of a story. There's a lot to teach in this one standard!

To help organize the unpacking process, we create tables for each standard that include the identified verbs and nouns or noun phrases (see Figure 3.1 for an example). When we use this process to unpack standards, we list all of the standards for our grade level and then work to identify what students need to understand (nouns) and do (verbs)—a process which in turn suggests teaching points, objectives, and eventually purpose statements.

Pacing Guides

Once you've compiled a list of verbs and nouns or noun phrases, you can turn to identifying goals and objectives. Even a cursory analysis of the standard related to texts in different media suggests that it will require several days, if not weeks or years, for students to master this content. When such is the case, teachers should develop pacing guides to ensure that standards are taught in a sequence that makes sense and that content knowledge develops throughout the year. Writing a pacing guide takes time and is probably better completed by groups of teachers to ensure that the plan is as comprehensive as possible. Pacing guides are not meant to be scripts, but rather blueprints for what to teach

Figure 3.1

Verbs and Nouns in Common Core State Standards

Grade/Subject	Standard (What Students Will Do)	Verbs (How Students Will Demonstrate Their Understanding)	Nouns (What Students Are Required to Know)
Grade 11–12/ Speaking and Listening	Respond thoughtfully to diverse perspectives; synthesize comments, claims, and evidence made on all sides of an issue; resolve contradictions when possible; and determine what additional information or research is required to deepen the investigation or complete the task.	Respond Synthesize Resolve Determine Deepen Require Complete	Perspectives Comments Claims Evidence Contradictions Information Research Investigation Task
Grade 10/Geometry	Prove that all circles are similar.	Prove	Circles
Grade 9–10/Reading Literature	Determine a theme or central idea of a text and analyze in detail its development over the course of the text, including how it emerges and is shaped and refined by specific details; provide an objective summary of the text.	Determine Analyze Provide Emerge Shape Refine	Theme Central idea Details Summary
Grade 9–10/Literacy in Science	Follow precisely a complex multistep procedure when carrying out experiments, taking measurements, or performing technical tasks, attending to special cases or exceptions defined in the text.	Follow Take Perform Attend Carry out	Procedure Experiments Measurements Technical tasks Special cases Exceptions

(continued)

Figure 3.1

Verbs and Nouns in Common Core State Standards (continued)

Grade/Subject	Standard (What Students Will Do)	Verbs (How Students Will Demonstrate Their Understanding)	Nouns (What Students Are Required to Know)
Grade 8/ Mathematics	Solve linear equations with rational number coefficients, including equations whose solutions require expanding expressions using the distributive property and collecting like terms.	Solve Include Require Use Collect	Linear equations Rational number coefficients Distributive property Like terms Expressions
Grade 6–8/Literacy in History and the Social Sciences	Determine the central ideas or information of a primary or secondary source; provide an accurate summary of the source distinct from prior knowledge or opinions.	Determine Provide	Central ideas Primary source Secondary source Summary Prior knowledge Opinions
Grade 4/Reading Literature	Compare and contrast the point of view from which different stories are narrated, including the difference between first- and third-person narrations.	Compare Contrast	Point of view Stories Narrations
Grade 2/ Mathematics	Mentally add 10 or 100 to a given number 100–900, and mentally subtract 10 or 100 from a given number 100–900.	Add Subtract	Number
Grade 1/Writing	Write narratives in which they recount two or more appropriately sequenced events, include some details regarding what happened, use temporal words to signal event order, and provide some sense of closure.	Write Sequence Recount Use Signal Provide	Narratives Events Details Temporal words Closure

and when to teach it. Unfortunately, rigid interpretation of pacing guides has resulted in highly scripted curricula that are not
responsive to the needs of individual students (Au, 2007).

Concerns about pacing guides are well-founded, as their development and use have varied widely. Many educators report that
the introduction of pacing guides causes them anxiety (David,
2008). Such concerns are almost always due to the design of the
pacing guides being used: Instead of keeping the user in mind,
pacing guides too often fail to address the very real likelihood
that the amount of time spent on particular aspects of the curriculum will vary widely among different teachers and groups
of students—variances that cannot be predicted in advance.

Those charged with developing the pacing guides also face the
Sisyphean task of squeezing too many standards into a linear,
180-day timeline. A major criticism of state standards around
the country is that there are too many, they are too broad, and
they force teachers to make difficult choices about what will
and will not be taught. As a result, state testing frameworks
are used to narrow the curriculum to the content that is most
likely to appear on the test (Darling-Hammond, 2004).

Yet pacing guides do help with planning, time management,
and continuity across schools. In addition, they can be used to
detail resources and materials that some teachers might not be
familiar with. As an example, Figure 3.2 shows a pacing guide
that was based on the analysis of the standard we previously
discussed (comparing and contrasting print and nonprint versions of the same narrative). This type of pacing guide does not
include specifics about what has to be taught when, but rather
focuses on a number of objectives that should be accomplished
in order for the standard to be met. It also includes ideas for

Figure 3.2

Sample Pacing Guide for English 7

Theme, Project, Problem, or Question: How does the medium affect the message?

Content Standard: Compare and contrast a written story, drama, or poem to its audio, filmed, staged, or multimedia version, analyzing the effects of techniques unique to each medium (e.g., lighting, sound, color, or camera focus and angles in a film).

Timeline: 10 instructional days

Objectives	Instructional Routines	Suggested Texts and Resources	Assessments
1. By the second day of instruction, students will identify similarities between two different versions (print and nonprint) of the same narrative text.	1. Teacher modeling of similarities and differences between versions of the same narrative.	1. Film versions from Canadian teaching website (www.filmlit.ca).	1. Quiz on similarities between two versions of the same narrative.
2. By the fourth day of instruction, students will identify differences between two different versions (print and nonprint) of the same narrative text.	2. Group work focused on similarities between two versions.	2. Dr. Martin Luther King Jr.'s "I Have a Dream" speech in print and audio recording (www.americanrhetoric.com/top100speechesall.html).	2. Constructed response assessment on differences between two versions of the same narrative.
3. By the sixth day of instruction, students will recognize, by technical name, techniques used in various mediums.	3. Group work focused on differences between two versions.	3. Audio and print versions of "Stopping by Woods on a Snowy Evening" by Robert Frost.	3. Practice sheets on techniques used in multimedia.
4. By the eighth day of instruction, students will analyze the effects of techniques unique to a specific medium and the impact the technique has on their understanding of the narrative text.	4. Independent practice assignment using two versions, one focused on similarities and one focused on differences.	4. Print and video versions of Janet Tashjian's *Tru Confessions* (1997).	4. Compare and contrast essay.
5. By the tenth day of instruction, students will compare and contrast two versions (print and nonprint) of the same narrative text using the techniques unique to each medium.	5. Treasure hunt on techniques used in multimedia using Internet resources.	5. Print and video versions of the Langston Hughes's short story, "Thank You, M'am" (2002).	
	6. Teacher modeling of composing process for a compare and contrast essay.	6. Glossary of film terms in John Golden's *Reading in the Dark: Using Film as a Tool in the English Classroom* (2001).	
	7. Students choose from a list of films (with parent permission) to compare and contrast print and film versions.		

instructional routines, materials, and assessments. Again, it's a guide rather than a script, and teachers are encouraged to use it as a starting place for developing their lessons. The pacing guide provides the fodder that teachers need to establish and communicate the purpose each day to their students.

David (2008) reminds us that the effects of pacing guides "depend on their design and how district and school leaders use them. The best pacing guides emphasize curriculum guidance instead of prescriptive pacing; these guides focus on central ideas and provide links to exemplary curriculum materials" (p. 88). That's our belief as well. Pacing guides should be used to focus on central ideas and resources so that teachers can determine the purpose of every lesson.

Unpacking standards provides the content component of the purpose; now it's time to turn our attention to the language component.

The Language Component

A challenge for all learners, especially for those learning English, is that the talk of school is decontextualized—that is, it requires students to discuss events, objects, and people that are not present. This "decontextualized discourse relies heavily on the language itself in the construction of meaning," and students must use highly conceptual vocabulary to make themselves understood in the classroom (Justice, 2006, p. 66).

Although many students benefit from clearly stated purposes, it appears that English language learners are especially sensitive to them—after all, they are less able than native English speakers to process verbal and written directions in English

(August & Hakuta, 1997). Ensuring that the purpose of a lesson is as clearly stated as possible can mitigate such challenges.

In content areas such as mathematics, science, and physical education, stating the language demand of a given task has proven effective at helping students learn content (Carrier, 2005; Clancy & Hruska, 2005; Hudson, Miller, & Butler, 2006). Additionally, Echevarria, Short, and Powers (2006) found that analysis of the language demand of a task, paired with stated purposes of written and verbal language production, resulted in higher levels of achievement for English language learners.

Communicating a language purpose is important because *all learning involves language*. Across learning contexts, students use language to think. While they are doing content work—whether it's math, science, social studies, or art—students are also reading, writing, speaking, and listening. Whereas the content purpose is fairly easy to identify from standards, the language purpose isn't always readily apparent. That's because the language purpose requires an understanding both of the content and of the linguistic needs of the students in the class. Two classrooms teaching the same content may have different language purposes due to the different needs of the students.

We analyzed 500 examples of language purpose statements submitted by teachers and identified three general categories of statements: vocabulary, language structure, and language function. Figure 3.3 contains examples of statements in each category.

Vocabulary

Vocabulary is one category that teachers can use to identify the language component of their purpose statement. The size of a

Figure 3.3

Examples of Language Purpose Statements

Content Area	Vocabulary	Structure	Function
Mathematics	Use *less than, equal to,* or *greater than* to compare groups or numbers.	Highlight addition signal words in a word problem.	Describe the relationship between numbers in expanded form and standard form.
Social Studies	Name the routes and explorers on a map.	Sequence the steps of food production using the signal words *first, then, next,* and *finally.*	Justify in a paragraph the ways fire was used for hunting, cooking, and warmth by citing three examples.
Language Arts	Use *who, what,* and *why* to ask a question of your partner.	Identify the verb tenses used in the reading to explain what happened long ago, and what will happen in the future.	Explain what organizational pattern was used by the writer and critique its adequacy.
Science	Label a diagram of the digestive system (*teeth, mouth, esophagus, stomach, small intestine, large intestine, colon*).	Using the sentence frame "On the one hand, _____. On the other hand, _____," students will demonstrate their knowledge of the Earth's layers.	I can inform my team members about three ways that an environment can change.

Source: From "Unpacking the Language Purpose: Vocabulary, Structure, and Function," by Doug Fisher and Nancy Frey, 2010, *TESOL Journal,* 1(3), pp. 315–337. Copyright 2010 by TESOL. Adapted with permission.

student's vocabulary is among the greatest predictors of how well he or she will understand a given text or lesson (Baker, Simmons, & Kame'enui, 1998; Carlo et al., 2004). The relationship between vocabulary and comprehension is so powerful that there is evidence that vocabulary size in kindergarten is an effective predictor of reading comprehension in the later school years (Scarborough, 2001). To understand a vocabulary term, students must also learn the concept behind it, as well as all of the words used to define the word (Brown, 2007). These terms are often identified within the content or grade-level standards. Vocabulary knowledge is especially important for English language learners; indeed, much of the current research on such students has focused on the best ways to develop their general word knowledge, academic terminology, and ability to learn new words that represent unfamiliar concepts (Nation, 2001).

Specialized Versus Technical Words

Within the broad category of vocabulary, two subcategories are useful in determining students' needs: *specialized* and *technical*. Specialized words are defined as words whose meaning is altered by the context or discipline (Vacca & Vacca, 2007). For example, the words *tissue*, *vessel*, *petrified*, and *culture* all have multiple meanings. A high school science teacher might therefore establish as a language purpose that students understand the meanings of these words in the context of studying the human anatomy. Examples of language purpose statements that address specialized vocabulary include the following:

- Distinguish between the common and social studies–related meanings of *constitution*, *right*, and *pact*.
- Use the correct version of *rod* and *cone* when discussing the eye.
- Clarify the meaning of *light*, *perspective*, *line*, and *shape* as related to visual art.

In addition to ambiguous words, specialized vocabulary also includes words for which students know some part of the meaning, but have not yet mastered their full complexity. For example, students might understand the common meaning of the word *run* but not understand how the word is used in relation to computer programming or auto mechanics.

Unlike specialized words, technical words have a single definition and are typically used in only one discipline (Vacca & Vacca, 2007). *Mitrochondria*, *saxophone*, and *foreshadowing* are all examples of technical terms that are strongly associated with a specific content and have only one meaning. It should be noted that all disciplines use a mix of both technical and specialized vocabulary. Consider the following purpose statement:

> Employ scientific vocabulary related to seed dispersal during partner conversations.

The vocabulary in this case could include a technical term such as *dispersal vectors*, but also a specialized term such as *gravity*. Here's another example:

> Use mathematical terms (*solid figure*, *angle*, *vertices*, *face*) to explain why answers are reasonable.

In this case, *solid figure* and *vertices* are technical words, while *angle* and *face* are specialized terms.

Language Structure

Although learning about English language structure is important for all students, English language learners in particular need a lot of practice to help them internalize common forms. Such learners do not develop oral, reading, or writing proficiency by simply being exposed to the language (Palumbo & Willcutt, 2006). Teachers establish purpose related to language structure in four ways: through grammar and syntax rules, signal words, sentence frames for scaffolding language usage, and the teaching of idiomatic expressions.

Grammar and Syntax. Although the content of most lessons is not focused on grammar, there are times when grammar can be highlighted as part of the language purpose for a lesson. For example, in a 2nd grade science lesson on the life cycle of a frog in a class made up predominantly of English language learners, the language purpose might highlight the use of past tense verbs. Such was the case in the class of Ms. Cortez, a teacher of our acquaintance; she told us that she highlighted the past tense to "provide corrections as students used language because the purpose was public and students knew that it was about practice, not being embarrassed." This approach is consistent with the evidence that explicit corrective feedback results in improved proficiency (Ellis, Loewen, & Erlam, 2006), yet is sensitive to the experiences that some students have from the correction and feedback process (Loewen et al., 2009).

Here are some other examples of grammar- or syntax-related language structure purpose statements:

- Use past tense regular verbs to discuss the lab experiment.
- In complete sentences, retell the main ideas from the film to a partner.
- Identify subject/verb agreement errors in the group's draft presentation.

Signal Words. Signal words are the signs or markers that English speakers and writers use to let listeners and readers know what is coming next. These are often misused (if they are used at all) by English language learners, who may be familiar with basic signal words such as *but* and *because* but not with more complex signal words, especially those that appear more frequently in writing, such as *moreover* and *nevertheless*.

When comparing and contrasting, signal words are helpful in maintaining the structure of spoken or written text. Examples include *although, as well as, as opposed to, both, but, by contrast, compared with, different from, either/or, even though, however, in common, in comparison, instead of, like, on the other hand, otherwise, similar to, similarly, still, unlike, whereas,* and *yet*. Many signal words are also helpful in denoting chronological order, including *after, afterward, another, as soon as, before, during, finally, first, following, immediately, initially, last, later, meanwhile, next, not long after, now, on (date), preceding, second, soon, then, third, today, tomorrow, until,* and *when*. Here are examples of purpose statements related to signal words:

- Retell the steps in the life cycle of a butterfly using chronological-order signal words (e.g., *first, next, then,* and *finally*).
- Use the "if . . . then" structure to describe cause and effect.
- Compare and contrast two versions of the same fairy tale using signal words such as *contrast, in common, compared with, likewise, both, similarly,* or *although*.

Sentence Frames for Scaffolding Language Usage. Sentence frames allow teachers to scaffold students' use of academic English and increase the lexical density of their speech and writing. College composition experts Graff and Birkenstein (2006) recommend the use of frames (which they call "templates") as an effective way to develop students' academic language skills:

[E]ven the most creative forms of expression depend on established patterns and structures. Most songwriters, for instance, rely on a time-honored verse-chorus-verse pattern, and few people would call Shakespeare uncreative because he didn't invent the sonnet or dramatic forms that he used to such dazzling effect. . . . Ultimately, then, creativity and originality lie not in the avoidance of established forms, but in the imaginative use of them. (pp. 10–11)

Here are examples of purpose statements that refer to sentence frames:

- Use the frame "Some spiders _____, but all spiders _____" to describe information found in a text.
- Apply a frame (e.g., "What will your _____ do on _____?") in conversation lines.
- Present both sides of an argument to a peer using the frame "On the one hand, _____. But on the other hand, _____."

Idiomatic Expressions. In addition to emphasizing grammar, language purpose statements can emphasize idiomatic expressions and figurative language. We include idiomatic expressions and figurative language as a form of structure (rather than vocabulary) because they are most commonly used as phrases or complete sentences rather than as words and terms. In addition, they often serve as a frame for establishing an idea or concept, and therefore influence longer written passages and conversations.

Language Function

Halliday (1973) lists seven categories of language functions: instrumental, regulatory, interactional, personal, imaginative,

heuristic, and representational. He argues that these functions represent the various ways that humans use language
with one another. Language functions can be translated into
verbs related to classroom interactions and expectations for
student performance. For example, Bailey and Butler (2002)
found that the following language functions appeared in
several state science content standards: *analyze, compare,
describe, observe,* and *record.* Common language functions
useful in school contexts include the following: *express an
opinion, describe, summarize, persuade, question, entertain,
inform, sequence, disagree, debate, evaluate,* and *justify* (Newmeyer, 2000). Here are some examples of purpose statements
that include language functions:

- Summarize the meaning of "taxation without
  representation."
- Question your partner about his or her creative
  writing.
- Persuade your reader to change a habit.
- Inform your listener about a current event.
- Justify your solution to the problem.
- Debate the merits of cloning animals.

To ascertain the appropriate language components that they
should address in their purpose statements, teachers must
understand the instructional needs of their students as well as
the linguistic demands of the content being studied. A variety
of different language purpose statements can be developed for
very similar content and standards. For example, for a lesson
in which students are expected to identify the phases of the
moon, any of the following language purpose statements could
be appropriate, depending on the component that the teacher
wishes to emphasize:

- Name the phases of the moon. (Vocabulary)
- Use sequence words (e.g., *first, then, next, finally*) to describe the phases of the moon. (Structure)
- Explain how the moon, earth, and sun move through the phases. (Function)

Making Connections Between Content and Language Components

As we have noted, there are a number of different ways to ensure that students understand that there are two components of each purpose, content and language. Sometimes, the content and language components are written separately; other times, they're written as a single phrase. It probably doesn't matter much. What does matter is that the students understand the purpose.

Let's examine an example of a teacher who successfully integrated content and language components into her purpose statements. In Ms. Matheson's 6th grade classroom, students focused on the following Common Core State Standard:

Understand that positive and negative numbers are used together to describe quantities having opposite directions or values (e.g., temperature above/below zero, elevation above/below sea level, credits/debits, positive/negative electric charge); use positive and negative numbers to represent quantities in real-world contexts, explaining the meaning of 0 in each situation.

Ms. Matheson's team unpacked this standard, identifying the verbs and nouns that indicate what students should know and be able to do. The team noticed that the standard employed the verbs *understand* and *use*, requiring the teachers to define ways to assess students' mastery of the content. The team also noted that the standard requires students to focus on *opposite directions* and *positive and negative numbers*. Unpacking the standard led the team to draft several objectives, including the following one:

> By the end of the week, as measured on the benchmark assessment, the student will be able to add and subtract positive and negative numbers representing authentic situations in which opposite directions or values are required.

Given that the standard was designed to provide students an opportunity to apply and extend previous understandings, Ms. Matheson developed a quick assessment to determine whether her students had the necessary background knowledge to meet the standard. She asked students to define, in writing, the phrases *positive number* and *negative number,* and to provide three examples of each. She also asked students to add positive and negative numbers in various combinations (e.g., $-9 + 4$, $15 - 27$, $-77 - 28$). The students did very well on the background knowledge assessment, indicating that they were ready to extend their understanding. Had they not done well on this assessment, Ms. Matheson would have spent time reviewing the prerequisite information, attempting to identify errors, misconceptions, and partial understandings that were interfering with her students' performance.

The purpose statements that Ms. Matheson developed out of the objective identified by her team can be found in Figure 3.4. These three examples do not represent consecutive days, but rather three different lessons designed to ensure that students

Figure 3.4
Ms. Matheson's Purpose Statements

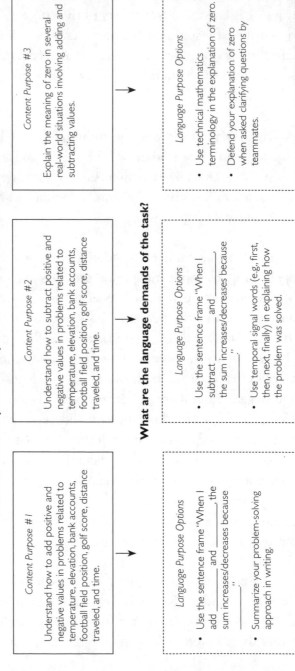

Content Standard: Understand that positive and negative numbers are used together to describe quantities having opposite directions or values (e.g., temperature above/below zero, elevation above/below sea level, credits/debits, positive/negative electric charge); use positive and negative numbers to represent quantities in real-world contexts, explaining the meaning of zero in each situation.

What can be accomplished today as we move toward the content standard?

Content Purpose #1

Understand how to add positive and negative values in problems related to temperature, elevation, bank accounts, football field position, golf score, distance traveled, and time.

Content Purpose #2

Understand how to subtract positive and negative values in problems related to temperature, elevation, bank accounts, football field position, golf score, distance traveled, and time.

Content Purpose #3

Explain the meaning of zero in several real-world situations involving adding and subtracting values.

What are the language demands of the task?

Language Purpose Options

- Use the sentence frame "When I add _____ and _____, the sum increases/decreases because _____."

- Summarize your problem-solving approach in writing.

Language Purpose Options

- Use the sentence frame "When I subtract _____ and _____, the sum increases/decreases because _____."

- Use temporal signal words (e.g., first, then, next, finally) in explaining how the problem was solved.

Language Purpose Options

- Use technical mathematics terminology in the explanation of zero.

- Defend your explanation of zero when asked clarifying questions by teammates.

grasped the concept. The content components of the purpose statements focus on specific aspects of the objective that students need to understand, whereas the language components focus on the linguistic demands of the task that students need to accomplish. Together, these two components ensure that student work is aligned with a grade-level-appropriate standard.

Conclusion

There are multiple purposes for each instructional event. If teachers were simply to focus on content, language learning would occur only incidentally; if teachers were to focus only on language learning, content understanding would not be likely to develop. These two components really do go hand in hand, as learning is based in language. All of us learn content as we read, write, speak, and listen. Accordingly, students' attention needs to be drawn to both the content and language expected of them. When students are alerted to the purpose and know what to pay attention to, they learn to use language academically.

As we have demonstrated, identifying the purpose of a lesson requires an understanding of the content standard, which is accomplished by unpacking the standard and creating pacing guides. Identifying the purpose also requires teachers to understand the linguistic demands of the task at hand and determine whether students need to focus on vocabulary, language structure, or language function.

4

Ensuring That the Purpose Is Relevant

We can't even begin to count the number of times we've heard that what we teach in school should be relevant to students' lives outside of school. People not in the education field will often ask, "Will students need to know this in the real world?" We would like to point out that school *is* the real world for millions of students and their teachers every day, and that we are preparing students for their possible futures, not necessarily the present. In doing so, we often teach things that students don't consider relevant. Trying to make every complex idea immediately relevant to the lived experience of a 12-year-old cheapens the experience and trivializes the value of learning for learning's sake. We do think that it is our job to make the curriculum relevant, but that may or may not involve making connections to the world outside of the school. Sometimes relevance is achieved when students take pride in understanding something about the biological, physical, or social world around them, or when students learn about their own learning habits. The Common Core State Standards make the case that relevance really means that teachers are focused on the knowledge and skills students need for success in college and careers. If it is true that teachers today are preparing students for jobs that don't even exist yet, why are we so worried about making sure that every part of our curriculum connects to students' experiences now?

There are multiple ways to make the curriculum relevant for students; drawing connections to the world outside of school is just one of them. To be clear, there are times that it is appropriate to ensure relevance by helping students understand that the information or skill has application in their lives. We heard this when a geometry teacher established the purpose related to learning about mid-segments of triangles. As she told her students, "Volcanologists use this information all of the time to determine the size of volcanoes." She also noted that if you're building a set for a play, you'll use triangle mid-segments to make sure everything is to scale. Both of these statements were attempts to make learning relevant for students by appealing to the "real world" outside of the school.

Beyond connections to the students' life outside of school, relevance can be attained when students have the opportunity to follow their own processes, not just learn facts and isolated skills. Doug remembers his 9th grade humanities class and the way that the teachers organized themes and allowed students to ask questions and then find the answers to those questions. In one unit, Doug's team decided to read *Spoon River Anthology* (Masters, 1915) in response to the theme "Matters of Life and Death." No one on the team remembers why this book was selected. There was no relevance between this collection of epitaphs about fictional people who lived in Illinois at the turn of the century and the life of a 14-year-old living in Southern California. Nonetheless, this group of students read the book and produced a play based on it. They still remember the characters who told the truth about their lives, without fear of consequences, and the façades these characters created while alive. The relevance of following his own process led Doug to a book and a set of ideas that he might otherwise have never known and that he drew on later in life—first in a college essay, and then again in a book for teachers.

Another way that we can ensure relevance is by providing students with opportunities to learn about their own learning processes. We all hope to know ourselves better and jump at chances to do so. Nancy was provided such an opportunity when she was in middle school. Though she had always been a good reader, she didn't really understand her own reading comprehension processes. Not knowing what to do with her all day, her teachers asked her to peer-tutor younger students. They didn't talk about the relevance of this request; they simply assigned her to a primary grade classroom. During that time, Nancy remembers coming to terms with her reading comprehension processes, realizing that not everyone used the same processes she did. Again, relevance was revealed years later, when Nancy became a teacher.

The issue of building relevance is a tricky one, as students' lives vary so widely, and the world in which they live moves so quickly. In the midst of all of this, we sit thinking about how relevance and purpose are related. The curriculum we teach is influenced by the lived experiences of our students outside of school, and the ways in which we formulate our disciplines to further make relevance apparent to them.

The Real World 2.0

One measure of relevance in the eyes of our students is the way we do (or do not) incorporate technology into our classrooms. By demonstrating sophisticated use of technology in the classroom, we can show students how school today relates to the world tomorrow. The "real world" for students is changing at an alarming rate; the jobs students will have in the future will involve technology that we can't even imagine. Some make the case that today's students are digital natives, whereas their teachers are digital immigrants (Prensky, 2001)—students use iPads and smartphones to find information at home, but clunky desktop computers (or, worse, printed text) to find information at school. They subscribe to RSS feeds so that news finds them, while many of us read newspapers to find news.

One of the ways we can increase relevance for students is to encourage them to use their "real world" tools in class. What if schools did not ban cell phones and other electronic devices, and instead taught students how to use them for their learning tasks? Policies such as the one below from San Diego Unified School District (2003) would have to change:

> These devices [cellular phones, pagers, and other electronic signaling devices] must be kept out of sight and turned off during the instructional program. Unauthorized use of such devices disrupts the instructional program and distracts from the learning environment. Therefore unauthorized use is grounds for confiscation of the device by school officials, including classroom teachers. Repeated unauthorized use of such devices may lead to disciplinary action.

Instead of such a blanket prohibition on technology, schools might institute courtesy policies, such as the one from our own school shown in Figure 4.1. In our case, we teach students how and when to use their electronic devices. This approach increases the relevance of the material to students and makes them see their teachers and administrators in a more positive light. After all, the ability to access, analyze, and produce information for a digital society is an essential 21st century skill.

The National Assessment of Educational Progress (NAEP) is developing a test of technology literacy that will be administered beginning in 2012. A draft framework, which will form the basis for what is tested, was developed by the discussion group and released in July 2009. It includes the following objectives for students:

1. *Knowledge*
   - Understands the nature of technology in its broadest sense.
   - Knows how technology is created and how it shapes society and in turn is shaped by society.
   - Understands basic engineering concepts and terms, such as *systems, constraints,* and *trade-offs.*
   - Is aware of the various digital tools and their appropriateness for different tasks.
   - Understands cultural differences by engaging with learners of other cultures.

2. *Capabilities*
   - Uses a wide range of technological tools and systems, ranging from kitchen appliances and alarm clocks to cars, computers, cell phones, and the Internet.

Figure 4.1
Courtesy Policy

Courtesy is a code that governs the expectations of social behavior. Each community or culture defines *courtesy* and the expectations for its members. As a learning community, it is our responsibility to define *courtesy* and to live up to that definition. We must hold ourselves and one another accountable for interactions that foster respect and trust. Discourteous behaviors destroy the community and can result in hurt feelings, anger, and additional poor choices.

In general, *courtesy* means that we interact with one another in positive, respectful ways. Consider the following examples of courteous and discourteous behavior.

Courteous	Discourteous
• Saying "please" and "thank you" • Paying attention in class • Socializing with friends during passing periods and lunch • Asking questions and interacting with peers and teachers • Asking for, accepting, offering, or declining help graciously • Allowing teachers and peers to complete statements without interruptions • Throwing away trash after lunch • Cleaning your own workspace • Reporting safety concerns or other issues that require attention to a staff member	• Using vulgar, foul, abusive, or offensive language • Listening to an iPod during a formal learning situation (such as during teacher modeling or while completing group work) • Text messaging or talking on a cell phone during formal learning • Bullying, teasing, or harassing others • Hogging bandwidth and/or computer time • Not showing up for your scheduled appointments or completing tasks • Failing to communicate when you're not coming to school

- Can apply technological concepts and abilities creatively, including those of engineering design and information technology, to solve problems and meet goals.
- Communicates information and ideas effectively to multiple audiences using a variety of media and formats.

3. *Critical Thinking and Decision Making*
   - Collects and analyzes data to develop a solution to complete a project.
   - Uses multiple processes and diverse perspectives to explore alternative solutions.
   - Can evaluate product claims and make intelligent buying decisions.
   - Participates thoughtfully and productively in discussing critical societal issues involving technology, such as energy and power, climate change, and land use policy. (Section 1, pp. 4–5)

The discussion group promises to include extended response questions that measure a range of skills on the test. According to the draft framework,

> [Students] might be asked to construct a wind turbine from a set of virtual components in which there are several combinations of turbine blades and generators . . . select different types of graphic representations for the tabulated data they captured . . . interpret their data, make a recommendation for the best combination of turbine blade and generator, and justify their choice in a short written (typed) response. (pp. 4–6)

Consider the myriad skills needed to answer this item. Knowledge of science and mathematics is certainly key, but also the literacy skills needed to predict, confirm, monitor, evaluate, and justify the steps of the task. The NAEP's technology literacy framework is nothing less than a clarion call—learning in the 21st century can no longer be limited to parroting existing knowledge; it is truly about creating knowledge, and understanding the purpose for doing so.

How should classrooms be structured to ensure that the purposes we establish are relevant for students? The NAEP framework doesn't specify the tools that students need to know how to use. We imagine that they know the tools change rapidly, and specific ones can become rapidly outdated. (Note that the San Diego technology policy we quoted earlier mentions pagers, even though most of us haven't seen one in a decade.) The NAEP objectives focus on *function*, not tools; the needs to evaluate, analyze, and so on transcend the tools we use to do so. We classify these functions into four broad categories because we all *find, use, produce,* and *share* information (Frey, Fisher, & Gonzales, 2010).

Finding Information

We sometimes forget that students watch everything we do. Their vantage point allows them to observe and analyze the ways we respond to situations and solve problems. These unguarded moments reveal much to them about how we think. Chances are good that you use some pretty sophisticated means for locating information. Need to gauge what time to leave after school to make your dentist appointment? You might turn to Google Maps to figure out your path and estimate the time it will take to get there. Heard about the trade your favorite team made late last night? You might check the team's application that you downloaded on your smartphone. Yet rarely do these methods make it into the classroom curriculum. A research paper on Vikings means a trip to the school library to check out a book, even though the Wikipedia entry has the latest information about their possible use of sunstones (Iceland spar) to navigate long distances under cloudy skies. In fact, it is likely that Wikipedia is considered a suspect source of information, and students are told not to use it at all. Though the entries themselves may not be authoritative, the linked footnotes for most entries offer ways to verify or find further information on the content.

When students do get an opportunity to use Internet sources, they are likely to end up with bad or incomplete information because they have not been taught some simple methods for making searches more productive. These include learning search techniques such as putting quotation marks around phrases, or limiting searches to a particular domain name by adding the term "site:" before the word or phrase ("site:library of congress," for example, yields only information from the Library of Congress). Click on the Wonder Wheel option after a Google search, and related searches are shown in the form of a graphic organizer (see Figure 4.2). You may know of other methods as well; the point is that they need to be taught, not kept away from the classroom.

Using Information

Locating information is only the first step of research; students also need to know how to effectively use the information they find. The easy availability of digital information has blurred the boundaries of acceptable school practices. Complaints about plagiarism abound as students simply copy and paste text they find online. Responses to these incidents are typically swift and absolute—a zero on the assignment, often accompanied by other punishments that are delineated in the student honor code.

To be sure, there are cases where students willfully copy with the intent to deceive. But our experience has been that in

Figure 4.2

Wonder Wheel for Library of Congress Google Search

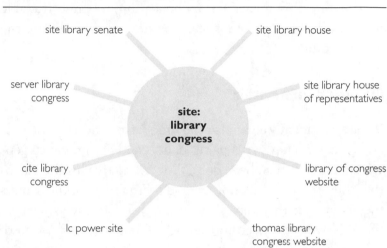

site library senate

site library house

server library
congress

**site:
library
congress**

site library house
of representatives

cite library
congress

library of congress
website

lc power site

thomas library
congress website

most cases, students aren't clear on what constitutes a violation. We're not talking about what has been discussed in class, or what's in the syllabus, but rather what the student actually understands about plagiarism. We rarely model what we want students to do with information once they find it. How often have all of us teachers used materials freely in our classrooms without properly citing them?

We have found the materials available at the Media Education Lab at Temple University (http://mediaeducationlab.com) to be very useful in teaching students and teachers about copyright and fair use in education. This website is chock-full of short videos, digital presentation materials, and helpful links for supporting students as they use information they find online. We use this material in an introductory unit on citing sources using Modern Language Association and American Psychological Association references. By grounding issues of plagiarism within media literary education, we are better able to establish the purpose for learning how to properly cite the works of others.

Producing Information

We are continually amazed at the innovative ways students create. Of course they write, paint, dance, and play music, as generations before them have done. But add to this list the videos that they produce, edit, and upload to YouTube, or the avatars they create for themselves for online role-playing games like *World of Warcraft*. Even in the more familiar (to us) world of Facebook, we have seen students shape their online identities such that we barely recognize them as the flesh-and-blood people we see each school day. Yet in the classroom, opportunities to create information are rare, even though many students are skilled at doing so.

A growing body of research is on the work of students using digital storytelling. Think of those Ken Burns documentaries on the Civil War, baseball, and jazz—those are examples of digital storytelling. Using still images, text, and voiceovers, the author presents information on a topic or tells an original story. Sylvester and Greenridge (2009) describe their work with struggling elementary writers who created digital stories. They state that there are seven elements of digital storytelling, derived from the work of Lambert (2002). Notice how the first five of the following elements mirror the ones we teach when writing traditional prose storytelling, while the final two are unique to the digital storytelling form:

1. *Point of view:* defining the specific realization that the author is trying to communicate within the story. Digital storytelling allows the storyteller to come close to his audience by expressing personal experiences through a first-person point of view.

2. *Dramatic question:* setting up a conflict from the beginning that will hold viewers' attention until the story is over. Similar to traditional storytelling, a plot is developed in a digital story, thereby distinguishing it from a slideshow of wedding pictures enhanced with music and flashy transitions.

3. *Emotional content:* dealing directly with the fundamental emotional paradigms such as love and loneliness, confidence and vulnerability, acceptance and rejection. Effective digital stories evoke an emotion from the audience, thereby validating the time and effort invested in the creation of the digital story. For the novice storyteller, laughter is a more commonly witnessed emotion.

4. *Economy:* consciously economizing language in relationship to the narrative. This requires the storyteller to be sensitive to the attentiveness of the viewing audience.

5. *Pacing:* determining the rhythm of a story to sustain an audience's interest.

6. *The gift of voice:* employing the pitch, inflection, and timbre of one's own voice to narrate the story is one of the most essential elements that contribute to the effectiveness of digital storytelling.

7. *Soundtrack:* using music to enhance the story and create an emotional response. (Sylvester & Greenridge, 2009, p. 287)

Sharing Information

It is difficult to separate the creation of information from the sharing of it, as these functions have become increasingly linked with the advent of digital technologies. Whereas students in the past would hang up a paper or do a presentation, students today can share in expanded ways that take up less physical space. Many teachers use classroom wikis to post work and promote discussion, for example. We frequently use the VoiceThread program (www.voicethread.com), which helps students create and share digital stories with the class; viewers of these digital stories can post their own comments and questions for others to see and listen to, thus promoting further discussion.

There are an increasing number of ways in which teachers can foster their growing ability to share information. For example, students can create their own podcasts using the recording capabilities available in most computers, or even develop their own avatars using the Voki website (www.voki.com). Fifth grade teacher Don Newton uses Voki for book reports. "My students make their own avatar and then write their book reviews," he told us. "The text is converted into speech, and then they upload the entire thing onto our class website. It's a protected site, so only my students and their families can view it. I really like how the parents can see their children's work and the work of others."

Our colleague Katie Smith, an 11th grade English teacher, started a project she calls Bookipedia. It's a classroom-based wiki website of books that students have read, with plot summaries and reviews. Some books have reviews from several students, offering a range of opinions and insights. Students looking for a new book to read can check out the reviews. This year, Ms. Smith has further expanded the database to include short movie trailers that the students have created on some of the books, thus providing students with both visual and written information about the titles.

Another teacher at our school, health teacher Annaleah Enriquez, uses Glogster (edu.glogster.com), "a collaborative online learning platform for teachers and students." On this password-protected website, students can create multimedia posters using images, text, and sounds. Ms. Enriquez had her students use the site to create posters summarizing the psychology theories of Maslow, Erikson, and Freud. The site allowed her students to take a virtual gallery walk of their classmates' work.

Building Relevance Through Curricular Organization

As teachers, we can choose to organize our curriculum around themes and interdisciplinary instruction, which require students to make connections between and among ideas. We can also organize our curriculum around problems and projects, which require students to investigate and inquire. Finally, we can organize our curriculum around essential questions, which require students to conduct research and find answers. In organizing our curriculum in these ways, the daily purpose becomes important, as students want to understand how ideas fit together and what they will have the opportunity to learn.

Themes and Interdisciplinary Instruction

Thematic instruction is possibly one of the most enduring means for organizing curriculum. Ever since John Dewey

(1902) advised creating lessons linked to common themes in order to create meaningful learning experiences, teachers have sought to do so. Dewey advocated this approach because

> It economizes the workings of the mind in every way. Memory is less taxed because the facts are grouped together about some common principle, instead of being connected solely with the varying incidents of their original discovery. Observation is assisted; we know what to look for and where to look. (pp. 28–29)

The popularity of this approach has waxed and waned in the last century, as educational focus has shifted back and forth between knowledge acquisition and knowledge performance. It is important to remember that with each shift in focus comes new understanding about effective practice and assessment. We recognize that units built on inconsequential ideas (such as Nancy's apple unit, discussed in Chapter 2) will yield inconsequential learning results. But units that are constructed with rigorous thinking skills and robust content in mind can foster deep understanding about worthy topics (Carnegie Council on Adolescent Development, 1989).

A renewed commitment to the thematic approach in the late 1980s led to the emergence of interdisciplinary instruction, which encourages students to examine a topic through the lenses of two or more subject areas. Teachers found this approach to be motivating because it allowed them to step beyond their assigned discipline to showcase how they understand a topic more broadly. For example, world history teacher Rich Van Atta and visual arts teacher Corita Reyes see Picasso's 1937 masterpiece *Guernica* through different lenses, examining the historical background of the painting as well as Picasso's use of color and composition. An interdisciplinary approach allows the teachers to impart to students both historical knowledge of the Spanish Civil War as well as an understanding of how Picasso used line, shape, form, and color to convey meaning, and permits students to see firsthand how the disciplines inform and enrich one another. In addition, this approach makes learning seem more relevant to students, since they see how it applies to more than one discipline— thus answering that age-old question, "Why do we have to learn this?" As Fathima, a student in both Mr. Van Atta's and Ms. Reyes's classes, remarked,

> We learned about visual analysis in Ms. Reyes's class, and how to look real closely at the way Picasso used straight and curved lines to make it seem real chaotic and all. And then in Mr. Van Atta's class, we had this visual analysis worksheet that we did in our groups. This time we looked at each quadrant and looked for symbols. Like, I hadn't really noticed the skull head in there. And Jeremy [another student] was talking about the bull. Mr. Van Atta told us that the bull is in lots of Spanish stories and stuff.

For this lesson, Ms. Reyes's purpose statement was as follows:

> Today we're going to focus on Picasso's use of lines. You'll explain through example how he used straight and curved lines to create lots of tension in his painting.

Mr. Van Atta's purpose read thusly:

> Today we're going to identify the political symbols in *Guernica* and figure out the messages the artist was sending to the world when he displayed it at the World's

Fair in 1937. This will help you understand why this painting caused so much controversy at the time. Then, you'll be able to debate how the major powers responded differently.

In each case, the purpose was shaped by the subject area, but the overall effect was for Fathima and her fellow students to build and consolidate their knowledge about how history and art affect each other.

Project-based Learning

Project-based learning (PBL) has become a popular means for organizing content learning, and examples of it abound across every discipline and grade level. These units of study often span multiple class sessions, as students work together in teams toward completion. There are two major types of project-based learning tasks: those that require investigation, and those that require performance. Investigative PBL tasks invite students to answer a question that is not easily answered, such as why some species survived a natural disaster while others did not (Reiser et al., 2001). Performance-based PBL tasks require students to publicly display and discuss what they have created, as when students use their mathematical skills to design a tile pattern for the courtyard at their elementary school (Frey, Fisher, & Moore, 2005). Well-known examples of PBL performances include the Model United Nations project and mock trials that put well-known fictional characters on trial.

Project-based learning is typically highly motivating and engaging for students, but as most of us have learned, a busy classroom is not always a learning one. Without structured experiences, PBL tasks can result in little true learning beyond the completion of the task and a poor ability to apply concepts to other learning contexts (Sherin, Brown, & Edelson, 2005). Given that a definition of true learning is the ability to use a skill when not otherwise prompted to do so, the inability to use information beyond the classroom is troubling.

The role of purpose statements is vital in project-based learning. Without a clear purpose in mind, students are likely to barrel headlong into the project without the ability to organize their learning. As Kanter (2010) notes, "Before science knowledge is constructed [in project-based learning], the learner must have a reason to learn it, thus creating a context in memory for integrating new knowledge, ultimately to build meaningful understanding" (p. 528). He advises that the sequence of lessons be designed to balance the activities with the instruction, especially in providing a need to learn new information, opportunities to apply it, and chances to see how the information may or may not work for completing the project. This final design element, which he calls "highlighting an incongruity" (p. 531), is a central feature in a related curricular approach called problem-based learning.

Problem-based Learning

Problem-based learning owes its origins to medical school training, where it was observed that students learned more content when they had a fictional patient to diagnose and treat (Barrows & Tamblyn, 1976). This approach quickly spread to other college disciplines, and then to K–12 schools. It immediately resonated with educators because of the obvious benefits of building relevance through real-world connections. In addition, problem-based learning outcomes suggest that students who engage in the process acquire deeper content knowledge, more sophisticated problem-solving abilities, and the capability of directing their own learning (Bellard, French, & Ertmer, 2009).

As with project-based learning, problem-based learning relies on a constructivist approach to knowledge building. Although many of the steps are the same and typically rely on investigation and performance as outcomes, it is the structure of the problem itself that is unique. The problem given to students is intentionally vague and ill-defined, so that students will need to wrestle with identifying what they need to know, how they will learn it, and how it will be applied. This feature is perhaps the one most closely aligned with its medical school origins, where doctors must diagnose and treat patients who do not know what is wrong with them and who may not accurately report their symptoms. This feature has also drawn criticism, as some have charged that the lack of structure is frustrating and too difficult for many students (Sweller, 1988). In addition, the primary role of the teacher in problem-based learning is one of facilitation rather than overt instruction, which can also be challenging for students who need more scaffolded instruction (Kirschner, Sweller, & Clark, 2006).

There are cognitive advantages, however, in devising experiences in which students are likely to confront initial difficulty. These experiences can serve as a priming mechanism for new learning—a process known as *productive failure* (Kapur, 2008). There is evidence that students who are unsuccessful with a task and then receive additional instruction outperform those who did not experience failure and follow-up teaching (Kapur, 2009). Perhaps some of the criticisms leveled at problem-based learning have more to do with the length of the unit, or the students' lack of collaborative skills. We advocate for brief experiences designed to build students' stamina for more sustained problem-based learning, and for lots of opportunities for scaffolded instruction, such as teacher modeling and guided instruction—an approach favored by others who have used problem-based learning extensively (Hmelo-Silver, Duncan, & Chinn, 2007).

Purpose statements in problem-based learning should be delivered using a "just-in-time" approach that moves students from observation and awareness to reflection and metacognition. These are the moments when students exclaim, "Oh, I get it!" after the teacher offers insight into what they are doing. When 8th grade science teacher Bill Linn remarked to a group of students who were stymied in their efforts to complete an electrical circuit in order to operate a model vehicle they had built, he provided them with the following purpose statement:

> The purpose of this is to figure out what an electrical circuit needs to be complete, and what can get in the way. You've been learning about insulators and conductors. Can you check your circuit again to see what might be getting in the way?

This purpose statement redirected the students' attention to a detail they had overlooked—they had failed to strip away the wire insulation at the point of contact with the battery. Within a few minutes, the students were cheering as their vehicle moved across the floor.

Essential Questions

Essential questions are not easily answered; they are designed to provoke thought, discussion, and research among students as they construct an informed response to them (Wiggins & McTighe, 2005). As with interdisciplinary instruction, the intent of essential questions is to cause students to think beyond the boundaries of a single discipline to address topics that are developmentally meaningful. This last point is important in designing essential questions, as what may be interesting to one age group may prove less so to another. For example, the following four schoolwide essential questions drove the 2009–10 curriculum at the high school where we teach:

- What is race, and does it matter?
- Can you buy your way to happiness?
- Who am I? Why do I matter?
- How do interactions affect your life?

Though these questions are interesting and appropriate for adolescents, they would not work well in an elementary school. Younger students might be better served by questions such as the following:

- What are different ways to count?
- How do living things change as they grow?
- Why did people begin to go west?
- How do I stay healthy?

No matter the level, essential questions should challenge students to create and evaluate information and drive them to seek out information in an attempt to find answers. Some questions require students to take a position and defend it (e.g., "Is there ever a time when the ends justify the means?"). Questions like this challenge students' thinking about moral and ethical issues across multiple disciplines (Jacobs, 2004). Other questions are more specific to a single discipline, as when our school asked students, "How do environment, culture, and beliefs affect a person's health?" To answer this question, students drew on their knowledge of history, science, and humanities, but used them to inform a project for their health course. Had they not been able to address this ultimately as a question of physical health, they would not have answered it correctly.

Essential questions, while useful, require an effective purpose statement to steer students' attention to the content you have intended for them to learn. A broad question like the one about health in the previous paragraph is interesting, to be sure, but a student writer can easily veer into other disciplines, never to return to the original purpose. Students need to understand that the overall aim is to explore health-related decisions and habits. We find it useful to provide a checklist to help students stay on track when answering essential questions. A copy of this checklist can be found in Figure 4.3.

Conclusion

In this chapter, we have focused on the importance of ensuring that students understand the relevance of the established purpose. If we as teachers have done our jobs well, students see the connections between what they are learning today and a theme, problem, project, or question that is meaningful and interesting. In doing so, students have opportunities to find, use, produce, and share information using a wide range of technology tools that they use outside of school. They also see connections between the established purpose and their own lives and what they are learning about themselves, and have opportunities to follow their own paths rather than just learning

Figure 4.3

Checklist for Essential Question Essay in Health

Essential Question: How do environment, culture, and a set of beliefs affect a person's health?

World History
❏ Explain how health is related to world history.
❏ Provide more than one example from Unit 2 of how world history has affected the environment, culture, and beliefs.
❏ Provide more than one example of how environment, culture, and beliefs affect our health.

Biology
❏ Explain how health is related to biology.
❏ Explain the role of genetics upon our health and its relationship to the environment (pollution, climate change, etc.)
❏ Explain how environment, culture, and beliefs affect your health and relate it to biology (provide several examples).

English
❏ Develop ideas fully and provide many supporting details.
❏ Ensure that material is highly organized.
❏ Introduce few or no spelling or capitalization errors.
❏ Use varied sentence structure and correct grammar and punctuation.

isolated skills or facts. Still, there are times that we focus on learning for learning's sake; in those situations, students understand that relevance relates to success in college and careers and participation in a democratic society. Of course, relevance requires the teacher to know the students. Making connections between students and curriculum requires knowledge—deep knowledge—of both.

5

Inviting Students to
Own the Purpose

In this chapter, we focus on inviting students to own the purpose of lessons. Purpose statements may be derived from standards, but they are more helpful when students assume ownership of them. Of course, there are times that students develop their own purposes for learning, but we are realistic enough to know that teachers have to establish the purpose regularly if students are to learn what is expected of them.

Extrinsic Versus Intrinsic Motivation

As teachers, we want our students to be motivated to learn content, but are often confused about how to get them to do so. We spend time in the faculty lounge saying, "I'm not sure what's wrong with that kid; he's just not motivated." Motivation is a complex topic and has been the focus of thousands of studies. A brief summary of the major theories of motivation can be found at the website www.changingminds.org. Each of these theories has, at its core, a focus on either extrinsic or intrinsic motivation.

Extrinsic motivation refers to influences that come from outside of the individual, such as money or grades. An extrinsically motivated student will work on a task even if he or she has very little interest in it, because the rewards associated with completing it are worth it, at least to the individual. Schools are filled with extrinsic rewards: We give smiley faces, stickers, and grades to extrinsically motivate students to complete tasks that they might otherwise not be interested in. Some have called for the elimination of extrinsic rewards due to the fact that some students begin to perform only when the rewards are present. Kohn (1999) argues that students will actually produce inferior work when they are enticed with grades or other incentives.

Although we agree that an exclusive focus on extrinsic motivation is not healthy, we also understand the realities of teaching. For example, we are required to give our students grades. Parents expect a summary of student performance, and colleges want to know whom to admit. We can work on changing these expectations and systems, but right now in our classrooms, we have to give grades. We don't have to make grades as big a deal as we do, and we can certainly focus on student understanding and feelings of accomplishment, but grades will remain with us for the foreseeable future.

We have enough experience in the classroom to know that some of our students don't feel very good about themselves and that they aren't likely to be intrinsically motivated (that is, motivated from within). We can build their intrinsic motivation by recognizing their efforts and successes. Some students come to us with high levels of intrinsic motivation; others do not. We see part of our job as building intrinsic motivation, and sometimes we have to do so through extrinsic motivation.

The student who comes to mind as we write this is Crystal, a 9th grader we've come to know. Her home life is less than stellar; suffice it to say that we would be surprised if she ever heard *thank you, well done,* or *I love you* at home. When we met her, Crystal was not motivated to do well in school. In fact, she did very little of what anyone could call schoolwork. Mostly, she looked angry and sat through class without speaking. During a guided instruction lesson several weeks into the school year, Nancy got Crystal to share her thinking about the book they were reading in class. When Crystal finished talking, Nancy said, "Thank you. That gives us something to think about. You seem to be identifying with this book. Your thinking is right on, and I hope you'll share more of your ideas with the class." We remember this because Crystal cried when Nancy finished complimenting her. That's not to say that this one interaction fixed everything for Crystal; we still have hard days. But praising her and rewarding her taught her that we care and that we notice. Of course, we understand that we have to be very intentional about our efforts and cannot rely solely on extrinsic motivation. Our goal is not to have students rely on extrinsic motivation, but rather to build their intrinsic motivation, and gradually transfer their motivation from us on the outside to them on the inside.

We have found Herzberg's (1959) two-factor theory to be useful in our work in understanding the balance between extrinsic and intrinsic motivation. Herzberg studied the workplace and concerned himself with job satisfaction. He noted that the factors that motivate people can change over their lifetimes, as we have all seen with children as they grow up. Importantly, Herzberg found that "respect for me as a person" was one of the top motivating factors across every stage of life. This finding has profound implications for the classroom, as it suggests that students are motivated when they sense that their teachers respect them. We can all remember a time when we perceived that our teacher did not respect us, and we can remember our behavior as a result of that perception.

Herzberg separated motivators from what he called hygiene factors. The things that motivate someone—challenging work, recognition for effort, increased responsibility, belonging— result in increased satisfaction and subsequently increased effort. The hygiene factors—so named because their presence will not make you healthier, but their absence can cause health deterioration—include status, rewards, benefits, and the like, and their absence can result in demotivation.

We find it useful to focus on motivation, because we understand that the work we provide students has to be motivating, relevant, and interesting. Our recognition of their efforts can also be motivating, as can their sense of membership and belonging and increased responsibility for learning. Having said that, we give grades and other rewards. We understand from Herzberg that this does not affect our students' motivation, but *not* giving the grade or reward could undermine it.

Fixed Versus Growth Mind-sets

Carol Dweck (2006) suggests that there are two different mind-sets, and that they can be influenced by interactions we have with others. People with a fixed mind-set believe that their abilities are based on innate qualities and that their successes and failures are based on how smart or skilled they are. People with a growth mind-set believe that their efforts will result in new abilities, and that failures offer an opportunity to improve their performance. Dweck suggests that we all operate somewhere on a continuum between the fixed and growth mind-set.

Mind-sets play an important role in education, because parents and teachers can influence students' thinking about their efforts. Students with a growth mind-set are likely to keep working even when they experience setbacks, whereas students with a fixed mind-set are likely to give up when they encounter difficulties. Consider the situation we observed in a 4th grade classroom where students worked collaboratively to solve problems of changing decimals to fractions. There were three students in each group, and they took turns solving the problems with numbers, words, and pictures. Alondra, Devin, and Marco had completed several of the problems before getting to .10.

"The decimal part goes on the top, without the period mark," said Devin, who was using words to solve the problem. "Then you put it over 100. So you get 10/100." Marco solved the problem with pictures, and had colored in 10 of the 100 shapes. Alondra solved the problem with numbers. Showing her work, she said, "I put 10 over 100 because .10 means 10 because you move the decimal two places."

The students were all satisfied with their answer, but when Devin checked the answer in the key, he reported that they were wrong—the answer was 1/10, not 10/100. "I don't get it," said Devin, putting his head down on the table. "We did it right." Clearly, Devin had a fairly fixed mind-set; his failure frustrated him to the point of giving up. Marco had more of a growth mind-set. "Remember what Ms. Avila said about reducing them if you could," he said. "Can we try that?" At this point, Alondra's growth mind-set kicked in. "Let's start over," she said. "C'mon, we can do this. We just forgot one part. 100 is really 10 x 10, so let's divide by 10 on the top and the bottom. Look, then we get 1/10, just like we're supposed to!"

Dweck (2006) notes that the interactions students have with adults can influence their mind-sets. When adults praise children for being smart, we reinforce a fixed mind-set. The following are examples of guiding students toward a fixed mind-set:

- Good job! You are very smart.
- Congratulations, you didn't even have to try.
- I guess you were just born talented.

When adults recognize students' *efforts*, however, we reinforce a growth mind-set. The following are examples of guiding students toward a growth mind-set:

- Good job! Your perseverance paid off.
- Wow, I can see that you really tried hard to complete this.
- You must have really practiced a lot. It shows!

In developing students' growth mind-sets, and reflecting on our efforts to move between extrinsic and intrinsic motivation, we are reminded that the comments we make can either build a student's identity and sense of self, or destroy it. Johnston (2004) suggests that we choose our words carefully, using external praise to build students' internal motivation. For example, instead of saying "I'm proud of you," we might say, "I bet you're proud of yourself." This rephrasing lets the student know that we recognized quality work and the effort that went into that work, and that the student should indeed be proud. In carefully choosing our words to develop students' intrinsic motivation, we not only reinforce a growth mind-set but we also teach students what it feels like to enjoy success.

Goal Setting

We've talked a lot about motivation and what a teacher can do to build students' success through systematic work on mindset. Of course, motivation requires a meaningful task—and for a task to become meaningful, students have to know why they are going to do it and what they will learn from doing it.

As teachers, there are times when we help students set individual goals. In doing so, we help them focus on things that they need or want to learn. When the going gets rough, we can refer back to the goals that students have developed for themselves to refocus them on the instruction at hand and reenlist their attention and interest. Some of our colleagues invite students to develop weekly or monthly goals that they can talk about during individual conferences. A sample goal-setting form can be found in Figure 5.1.

Ms. Flores had the students in her multimedia lab class fill out a form like the one in Figure 5.1. One of her students, George, had written that he was good at filming and planning shots, but needed to work on his editing skills. When Ms. Flores talked to George about his goals, she learned that he wanted to know how to edit videos so that he could post better ones on YouTube. Ms. Flores and George discussed all the other skills that went into editing in addition to technical skills, and how noticing language would be important.

Understanding George's goal was important for Ms. Flores as she planned her classes and her subsequent interactions with George. Inviting students to have individual goals doesn't mean that they are excused from the lessons designed for the class, but rather that we can make sure that our classes are

Figure 5.1

Goal-Setting Form

I am good at _____   I need to work on _____

_____   _____

_____   _____

My plan is to improve _____

_____

_____

I will do the following to improve: _____

_____

_____

People who will help me improve include _____

_____

_____

I will know if my plan is working because _____

_____

_____

If my plan doesn't work, then _____

_____

_____

My reasons for wanting to improve are _____

_____

_____

meeting individual students' needs. When George experienced frustrations with his learning and needed help persevering, Ms. Flores was able to use the goals he had set for himself to motivate and encourage him.

At this point, you might be thinking about the coach who gives players a pep talk before the big game. The pregame speech is designed to inspire victory; it's motivational and emotional. Perhaps you're thinking teachers should provide students with these types of pep talks before projects are due or tests are administered. The problem is that these speeches aren't that effective in and of themselves. When athletes listen to the pep talks, they compare their self-perceptions of their skills with the expectations of the coach. Sullivan and Strode (2010) argue that it would be better for the coach to "better understand the goal-setting process to maximize the motivational and self-confidence benefits that goals can provide, thereby enhancing performance" (p. 19). In other words, the pep talk would be more effective if the coach worked with each player to set goals that build confidence over time.

Like coaches who want the best for each player and the team overall, we can assist students in taking ownership of their learning through goal setting. There are several ways to involve students in this. In some cases, teachers provide students "a list of the learning targets they are responsible for mastering, written in student-friendly language" such that students understand the goals and want to work toward accomplishing them (Chappuis & Chappuis, 2008, p. 17). The basketball coach who says, "You can do crossover dribbles three times without looking. Let's work together on increasing that to five times" is doing just that. In this approach, students develop an understanding about their current performance level and can compare that with the teacher's expectations. For example, when Mr. McKee discussed the following learning target with the class—"Using technical language, describe the processes involved in composing, conducting, and performing music"—Michelle knew that she needed to focus on the conducting aspect, as she already had experience with composing music and regularly performed in local theaters.

Alternatively, students can work together to create classroom norms and indicators of quality work. In this approach, students examine anonymous examples of class work to gain greater understanding of the goals they have created. In doing so, the students begin "to hold a concept of quality work roughly similar to that of the teacher" (Shepard, 2005, p. 67). For example, Ms. Doyle's 5th grade students agreed on a goal related to writing: To write three to five paragraphs for each of the teacher's prompts, with a total of three or fewer mistakes. Although this goal was part of a larger unit on quality writing that addressed voice, transitions, and thesis development, Ms. Doyle's students decided to focus on length and errors. Largely because they themselves set the focusing goal, they were able to improve on both of these aspects of their writing.

Involving students in goal setting is an important aspect of establishing purpose. When students understand the goal, they grasp the daily purposes that lead to meeting the goal. It's like those Russian nesting dolls, one inside the other: The daily purposes we establish fit nicely inside the goals that we develop with our students. Together, these goals fit within a larger unit of study, which fits into the grade-level standards.

"I Can" Statements

As we have noted, using student-friendly language in purpose statements helps students understand what is expected of them and what they are going to learn (Marzano, 2011). Writing student-friendly learning statements simply involves beginning the purpose with an approachable phrase like "I can" or "I am learning to," defining uncommon words in an age-appropriate way, and including an action that can be observed (Stiggins, Arter, Chappuis, & Chappuis, 2004). We are especially taken with the rephrasing of purpose statements for students into "I can" statements, as suggested by Au and Raphael (2007). To our thinking, "I can" statements provide students an opportunity to engage in positive future thinking. It's kind of like the familiar self-help advice that encourages people to think about themselves in the future having accomplished the thing that they're trying to do now. There's even evidence that positive future thinking is effective for a wide range of situations, including overcoming depression and suicide (MacLeod et al., 2005).

Phrasing the purpose statement in a positive, future-oriented way lets students know what they will be able to do if they engage in the learning activities. They may not be able to perform the task or skill immediately, but thinking about it as a possible future accomplishment will likely increase their motivation and drive to do so. As Virgil said centuries ago, "They can because they think they can." (A sample list of "I can" statements can be found in Figure 5.2.)

When the 4th graders in Ms. Chapman's class were learning word problems and getting confused about what to do with them, Ms. Chapman reminded them of their knowledge of multiplication and division. After modeling how to solve one of the word

Figure 5.2

List of Sample "I Can" Statements

I can identify the differences between fiction and nonfiction texts.

I can predict what might happen in a story by considering what has already happened.

I can summarize the actions of the main characters and justify my views by referring to the text.

I can critique why the characters act in the way they do.

I can describe how an author uses language and how language affects the reader.

I can discuss messages, moods, feelings, and attitudes by reading between the lines and using deduction.

I can use the language features of a range of nonfiction texts to improve my understanding of longer texts.

I can describe and evaluate the styles of different writers, finding examples and justifying my interpretations.

problems for the class, she said, "I can recognize when a word problem involves multiplication or division." She invited students to try the next problem with their tablemates. Most of them recognized the need to multiply to solve the problem, and several students were overheard using the "I can" statement. As one of the groups shared their solution with the class, Ms. Chapman wrote the "I can" statement on the board and invited students to read it aloud with her. As they worked on the next several problems, Ms. Chapman joined different groups of students, providing prompts and cues to guide their learning. In each interaction, she asked the students in the group to repeat the "I can" statement to solidify their understanding of the process for solving these word problems and to see themselves as successful.

We see "I can" statements as one of the first steps in getting students to explain the purpose in their own words. When students understand the purpose, they can easily explain or demonstrate what they are learning and use words that are relevant and meaningful to them. As teachers, we just have to ask them about their learning.

Asking the Right Question

All this talk about students being able to explain the purpose in their own words is for naught if the adults fail to ask the right question. We freely admit to being guilty of asking the wrong questions ourselves, so by no means are we distancing ourselves from this fundamental error. A number of years ago, we were working with an elementary school that was building its capacity using a gradual release of responsibility framework of instruction as its professional study. The educators at the school were investing their time on the focus lesson portion of the model, including the need to establish purpose. Lots of attention had been devoted to crafting purpose statements that would spur student learning. Many teachers posted statements on their boards to further reinforce the practice.

We were visiting classrooms, accompanied by the principal and the reading coach. Our purpose was to look for patterns of practice to determine areas for further discussion. We entered a 3rd grade classroom that was well into a social studies lesson on Native American tribes of the area. Although we had not been there during the time the teacher spent establishing purpose, we could see evidence that it had been done. On the board was a purpose statement that read as follows:

> Our purpose is to understand how the Kumeyaay Indian culture was shaped by its environment. We'll summarize what we find out and share summaries with our partners.

When we came into the classroom, the students were working in small groups using a map of a museum garden they had
visited the day before that featured native plants. They also
had a visual glossary of objects created by the Kumeyaay using
these plants.

After we watched for a few minutes, Nancy asked the students in one group what they were doing. They immediately
launched into an animated explanation of their task, which
was to guess which plants could have been used to make the
objects featured in the pictures and explain their reasoning.
Now, you know eight-year-olds: no detail is too insignificant to
share. Their explanation took several minutes, and they inter-
rupted each other in their eagerness to answer.

Despite the students' enthusiasm, we were troubled by their
response. Nowhere was there any mention of the purpose
statement that was on the board. Finally, Doug asked, "But
what about the people and their environment?"

Silence. The students looked at each other, and then one said
in a tone that suggested that Doug must be really confused,
"Well, you didn't ask us what we were *learning,* you asked us
what we were *doing!*"

What's that expression about "out of the mouths of babes"?
There it was—the fundamental error that was obvious to the
3rd graders but not to us. How many times have any of us asked
a student, "What are you doing?" This question communicates
to our students that we value the business of completing tasks,
rather than the learning the tasks are designed to spur. It suggests that compliance and completion are more important than
the reason for the task itself. That day was the day we stopped

asking, "What are you doing?" and began asking, "What are you learning?"

Asking the right question provides us with information about students' understanding and ownership of the purpose of the lesson. When we asked Mr. Vaca's U.S. history students, "What are you learning?" they talked about the New Deal. Antonio said that they already learned about the three R's: relief, recovery, and reform. He also said that they were going to eventually answer the big question, "Would you take the New Deal?" Marcus added, "But today we're really learning more about liberal ideas and what happened after Roosevelt." Jasmine noted that the country really had to deal with the Great Depression and needed new laws to make sure that something like that didn't happen again. As she said, "That's the reform part, and we're learning that right now, how the laws were changed to make sure we didn't have another Depression."

When we followed up with a second question, "Why are you learning this?" the students each had personal reasons that they shared with us. Marcus said, "This is how the world works, with different groups holding on to power at different times. You gotta know this if you're gonna be successful." Jasmine had a different take, saying, "There were a lot of people without jobs, like right now. The laws from back then worked for a while, but then didn't work. That's what Obama is talking about now. We need new laws now, because there are lots of people who can't get a job." Antonio added, "What happens in the economy matters because it's more than jobs, it's about who gets to go to college, or gets a loan to buy a car or house, or finds out that their life savings aren't worth anything. If we don't understand this, then we will make the same mistakes and maybe even not be able to fix it. It's about knowing your past so that you can have a better future."

Conclusion

In this chapter, we focused on the need to involve students in understanding and owning the purpose. We discussed motivation and encouraging a growth mind-set, as well as how to ensure that purpose statements are presented in student-friendly language. We are reminded of a Mark Twain quote: "It's not the size of the dog in the fight, but the size of the fight in the dog." Ensuring that students understand and own the purposes for their learning builds students' "fight" for a quality education that is relevant to their futures.

6

Identifying Outcomes
Related to the Purpose

As teachers, we don't want to create learning activities that are unworthy of the time invested in designing and implementing them. Most of us can recall times in our own schooling when we engaged in dubious activities that in retrospect probably didn't deliver much learning. For example, Nancy recalls being in middle school in the months leading up to the 1972 presidential election conventions. Her history teacher had all the students draw 20,000 balloons in their notebooks, so that they could envision the balloons that would be released from the ceilings at the conventions. Much energy was devoted in class and out of school to filling notebook pages full of red and blue dots, each with a little black squiggly line. Although it's true that Nancy recalls the number of balloons three decades later, in retrospect that time and energy would have been better spent learning something about the process of choosing a presidential candidate. A mock convention held in class would have consumed no more time, but yielded much more robust outcomes. Meaningful tasks and robust outcomes are essential considerations in establishing purpose, and they are inexorably tied to each other.

Making the Task Meaningful to Students

Productive group work allows students the opportunity to clarify and refine their growing understanding of what they have been learning. Interactions with peers are critical for students, who can scaffold one another's learning. In keeping with the work of Vygotsky (1978), peers extend each other's cognitive "reach" into the zone of proximal development (ZPD)—Vygotsky's term for potential learning. However, if students are to reach their ZPD, they must interact with each other and with the task in a purposeful way. Too often, students do not understand the purpose of what they are doing when engaged in group work. Without a clear purpose, learning takes a back seat to compliance and task completion. We look for the following six quality indicators of productive group work to ensure that projects are meaningful to our students:

1. Complexity of task
2. Joint attention to the task
3. Argumentation
4. Language support
5. Group size
6. The role of the teacher (Frey, Fisher, & Everlove, 2009)

Taken together, these quality indicators signal that meaningful productive work is occurring. Let's examine each of the indicators using a biology lesson taught by one of our colleagues.

Tenth grade biology teacher Jeff Bonine's Critter Project is a weeklong assignment during which students consolidate what they know about habitats, organisms, cellular structures, natural selection, and adaptation. One day during the assignment, Mr. Bonine's students are immersed in the business of creating a new creature: In groups of three or four, they have designed a previously unknown animal, applying their knowledge of natural selection and adaptation. One group has devised a salamander that lives in saltwater. "Let's talk about that," Mr. Bonine offers. "How will your salamander process the salt intake?" When members of the group look at one another in confusion, the teacher continues. "Amphibians don't usually live in that environment, so let's meet to see if we can't work this out."

In another corner of the classroom, four students are creating a cell journal illustrating the structures of their creature's cheek, heart, sperm, and egg cells, using what they have learned from their study of anatomy and physiology. "Remember the sperm cells need flagella to move," Kristen reminds her group. "Ours is a viviparous [live-bearing] mammal, so the structure of the egg is bigger, so there are fewer of them," explains Antonio. As group members discuss the features, Maralyn draws and labels the cells.

Complexity of Task

The first indicator of whether productive group work is meaningful is the complexity of the task. At its best, the task should be a novel application of the concepts and skills that students have learned. This means that the group is not simply replicating what the teacher has already modeled for them. Duplication alone doesn't allow for opportunities to experiment with the concepts under investigation. Duplication also decreases the chance that the group might fail—and although failure is not a commonly stated goal, the truth is that error-free learning is unlikely to result in *robust* learning. Students need opportunities to try, and at times fail, in order to reach new understanding. Of course, failure alone doesn't result in learning, but repair does. That's why it is critical that students have the opportunity to try something again when they fail. This productive failure condition can result in shifting the learners' attention to what is needed to be successful (Kapur, 2008).

In Mr. Bonine's class, the group's initial attempt to devise an amphibian that lived in a saltwater environment met with failure. However, the result focused the group's attention on new information about osmosis and ion exchange, and the need for cell structures that can process increased levels of salt and decreased levels of oxygen. Due to the students' initial unsuccessful attempt, their misunderstanding of a concept was brought to light. The group began to realize that their creature would need a freshwater environment to survive and reproduce.

Joint Attention to Tasks and Materials

When the entire class is engaged in productive group work, the teacher is not able to be simultaneously present in each group. Therefore, it is important to be able to recognize whether the work is productive or not, especially from across the room. Joint attention to the tasks and materials serves as a good quality indicator during this phase of instruction. This means that the students' body language and visual gaze are routinely fixed on the task at hand. In addition, members of each group should move in ways that suggest coordinated and purposeful effort: The student who sits physically apart from the group with arms crossed and eyes fixed elsewhere is probably not working productively, and the task is probably not very meaningful for at least that student.

The language exchanges that the teacher overhears can also signal whether the group is productive or not. Conversations should be mostly on topic, and students should be asking questions of one another as well as offering personal opinions and conclusive statements. Most important, the teacher should listen for evidence of students synthesizing information, as this process propels them to refine their understanding. Such evidence provides further insight into whether students understand the purpose of what they are doing. When Antonio remarks on the nature of his group's mammal and the characteristics of its sex cells, he is synthesizing information from several knowledge bases. His synthesis statement provides his group members with the scaffold necessary to extend their cognitive reach.

Argumentation

To reach consensus, students engaged in productive group work need to challenge one another, but without arguing. They can disagree with one another, provide evidence to persuade, offer opinions, and change opinions based on the input of others. Teachers often establish group norms to regulate the social aspects of the work. These norms include instruction and teacher modeling of how to share successes and failures, decision making, turn taking, and active listening.

Mr. Bonine has found that modeling conflict management is especially important. Since the beginning of the year, he has modeled, demonstrated, and thought aloud on the following six aspects of resolving a disagreement in the group:

- Listening to the views of others
- Avoiding hurtful statements about others
- Stating your own view without becoming defensive
- Identifying personal concerns and acknowledging the concerns of others
- Accepting the group's decision graciously
- Resuming the task

"I think conflict management is one of the most important life skills I can teach the kids," he told us. "They're young adults who will need to work within groups all the time in college or on the job. If they can't resolve differences peacefully, they'll get excluded from lots of opportunities because no one will want to work with them. I'm teaching them more than biology. I'm also teaching them how to work with others."

Language Support

As we discussed in Chapter 3, the purpose, rhetorical language structure, and academic vocabulary of a task should be supported visually and verbally. Mr. Bonine routinely posts his purposes on the whiteboard so that students can refer to them throughout the task. Among the purposes he posted for the Critter Project was the following:

> Use what you know about natural selection, adaptation, cellular biology, and an organism's interaction with the environment to design a new creature. You will have an opportunity to review these concepts as you design a previously undiscovered creature.

Each day, Mr. Bonine draws students' attention to the vocabulary they will need, reminding them, for instance, that the text of the cell journal should include the words *homeostasis*, *organelles*, and *tissue*.

Mr. Bonine also posts sentence frames in the classroom so that students can use more sophisticated rhetorical structures in their written work. For example, a frame for the adaptation portion of the assignment reads as follows:

> Natural selection affected the frequency of the following traits in _____ due to _____. These traits included _____. The cause of this change can be attributed to _____. This allowed some members to survive because _____, while others perished due to _____. This led to primary selection of _____ because of a reproductive differential.

In addition, Mr. Bonine makes simple language supports available to students. "I color-code their task sheets each day during the project so they can find their work," he chuckled. "If they're missing something, I can tell them to look for the lime green paper, which seems to help them stay organized." He also posts a daily schedule with suggested times next to each task, and displays a timer that projects the elapsed time. The color-coded task sheets, daily schedules, and timer provide the groups with additional organizational structures that help them focus their work.

Grouping

Purposefully constructed groups should maximize the strengths of their members without magnifying areas of need. This means that the groups should be heterogeneous in nature, so as to prevent the relative impoverishment of one group's resources and a concentration of resources in another. If groups are to be constructed homogeneously, then it is the task itself that should be differentiated. Additionally, the group size should be limited to between two and five students so that meaningful interactions can occur. Our experience has been that we see more passive behavior on the part of some individuals in larger groups. And while we advise groups of two to five, that doesn't mean they must all be the same size; some students work better in larger or smaller groups, and the same task can often be accomplished by groups of varying size.

The construction of groups should be based on assessment information and observation of student knowledge and behavior. Mr. Bonine used previous assessment results to construct groups so that individual members represented a gradient of knowledge of the various topics. For example, Madalyn had a good grasp of cellular structures and was an asset to her group when they developed the cell journal, but she had not done as well on the adaptation unit. Kristen, another member of her group, had done well on the adaptation unit and was able to scaffold Madalyn's understanding of this important concept. Their group's creature was a large bird with a bony crest across the top of its skull, and had developed this trait because of the propensity of its males to fight during mating season. Kristen was able to clarify the role of secondary sexual characteristics of male animals with Madalyn and the rest of her group during the writing of the report, which used the paragraph frame that the teacher had provided.

The Role of the Teacher

This final quality indicator concerns the ways in which the teacher supports, facilitates, and guides learning during productive group work. Paying attention to the learning environment—including noise level, student movement, and material distribution—is important but insufficient. This is prime time to put the quality indicators we've just reviewed through their paces. Are students interacting in meaningful ways, as evidenced by verbal interactions? Do you see joint attention to tasks and materials? Are there other language supports that are going unnoticed?

In addition to assessing the progress of the groups, this is the time to deliver small-group guided instruction as needed. Mr. Bonine did this when he met with the group that was trying to create a saltwater salamander. He asked robust questions to check for understanding, then provided cognitive and metacognitive prompts to trigger background knowledge and spur the students to consider the cellular processes involved in osmosis. When they had difficulty with the details of ion exchange, he brought them over to a classroom poster illustrating the process. This cueing, which shifted students' attention to a source of salient information on filtration of salts, alerted the group to missing information. When Mr. Bonine saw that they needed more instruction, he provided a few minutes of direct explanation on the scarcity of amphibians in saltwater environments. The scaffolds he was able to offer during this guided instructional exchange gave the group the information they needed to repair and revise their project, thus turning productive failure into productive success.

When students have a meaningful task, they get to work and learn. Productive group work, designed as part of a larger instructional framework, requires that students actively construct meaning through their interactions with one another, their teacher, and the content. These tasks should focus on an outcome—what students produce that the teacher can assess.

Learning Outcomes

As Figure 6.1 shows, there are four main sets of factors that influence learning outcomes: societal, curricular, teacher-related, and student-related. Although some of these factors—particularly those in the societal set—lie outside our direct control as educators, there is much that we can influence, especially in areas related to instructional design and relevant curricula. What we may lack in larger influence we make up for with proximity to the learner.

The dialogue we engage in as we cultivate student learning can have a powerful influence. Hattie and Timperley (2007)

Figure 6.1
Factors That Influence Learning Outcomes

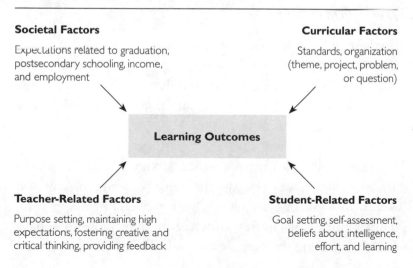

Societal Factors

Expectations related to graduation, postsecondary schooling, income, and employment

Curricular Factors

Standards, organization (theme, project, problem, or question)

Learning Outcomes

Teacher-Related Factors

Purpose setting, maintaining high expectations, fostering creative and critical thinking, providing feedback

Student-Related Factors

Goal setting, self-assessment, beliefs about intelligence, effort, and learning describe three processes present within these exchanges that answer the essential questions that all students have:

1. A *feed-up* process establishes the purpose and relevance of what is to be learned, answering the question, "Where am I going?"
2. A *feedback* process gives students information about their progress, answering the question, "How am I going?"
3. A *feed-forward* process scaffolds students' decision making about next steps, answering the question, "Where to next?" (p. 86)

Much of this book has been about the feed-up process, and we will discuss feed-forward in the next chapter. Right now, we'll direct our attention to feedback, as this is the process that provides students with a clear picture of their progress toward the learning outcomes of the lesson.

Types of Feedback

Students receive less feedback in schools than teachers often believe (Nuthall, 2005). This is perhaps due in part to the misconception that teachers are the only ones who can provide feedback, when in fact it can come from fellow students, or even be self-initiated.

It is important to define what feedback is *not*. It is not rewards—grades, smiley faces on papers, praise, or extra playtime at recess. Rewards undermine motivation and fail to supply students with useful metrics to determine how close they have come to meeting the purpose of a task (Kohn, 1999). Telling a young reader, "Good job!" leaves the student confused—what was "good"? Pronunciation? Fluency? Simple compliance?

In a summary of the research on the negative effects of feedback, Shute (2008) notes that the most counterproductive types of feedback include comments that are viewed as criticism or manipulation, comparing the student's grade to that of peers, vague statements, and interrupting students as they're problem solving. The best feedback, it seems, is formative in nature, occurring while students are learning, not after the fact. It is not a thinly veiled form of behavior management. Figure 6.2 illustrates the relationship between purpose and feedback.

Hattie and Timperley (2007) write about four distinct kinds of feedback that teachers can use with students: feedback about the task, feedback about the processing of the task, feedback about self-regulation, and feedback about the self as a person. Keep in mind that each of these kinds of feedback can have a negative effect if not done well. The most effective kinds of feedback offer students information about the processes they are using and encourage self-regulation.

Feedback About the Task. Feedback about the task—sometimes called corrective feedback—is the most common form of feedback. It is typically related to performance, such as reading aloud, playing an instrument, or finding the answer to a math problem. This type of feedback is usually related to the accuracy of the action.

Feedback about the task shouldn't be too lengthy or complex, as this can hinder the students' ability to complete the task

Figure 6.2
A Model of Feedback

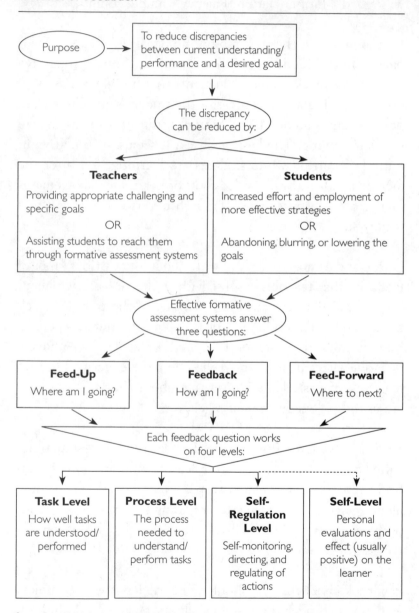

Source: From *Visible learning: A synthesis of over 800 meta-analyses relating to achievement* (p. 176), by J. Hattie, 2009, New York: Routledge. Copyright 2009 by Routledge. Reprinted with permission.

correctly—a long, complicated reply may confuse the student or cause him or her to stop listening (Balzer, Doherty, & O'Connor, 1989). Feedback that is too personal should also be avoided, as it might not contain enough information about the task (e.g., "You're so smart! You solved that equation correctly."). And feedback about the task alone, especially about an error, can result in a student's inwardly harsh assessment of self—"I'm too stupid to do this" isn't something we would encourage any student to say about himself. Burnett (2003) studied the relationship between teacher feedback and student self-talk among more than 700 students in grades 3–6 and found a strong correlation between negative self-talk and negative feedback.

The timing of the feedback within the instructional cycle is also important, as corrective feedback is at its most useful when the concepts or skills being learned are new. (If the student's main issue is a lack of knowledge, then all the feedback in the world isn't going to be helpful; the student needs to learn or relearn the necessary information.)

Feedback About the Processing of the Task. Feedback about the processing of the task is especially valuable, as it encourages the learner to think about "the construction of meaning (understanding) and relates more to the relationships, cognitive processes, and transference to other more difficult or untried tasks" (Hattie & Timperley, 2007, p. 93). This type of feedback consists of oral or written statements that draw the learner's attention to errors and suggest problem-solving strategies such as determining the importance of a passage, making connections to other texts and experiences, or visualizing. Strategies should be related to a breakdown in comprehension, not simply a set of steps to follow whenever reading.

Knowing how to put problem-solving strategies into play is representative of a deeper level of understanding, and providing learners with feedback that encourages them to do so will lead to new learning. When a teacher observes a student computing a math problem incorrectly and says, "Think about how you're going to get all the fractions into common denominators before you add them," he is drawing the student's attention to a strategy. This kind of feedback is likely to be more useful the next time the student adds mixed fractions than feedback about the task alone (e.g., "That answer is incorrect") would be.

Feedback About Self-Regulation. This type of feedback encourages students' metacognition and self-regulation of behavior, especially as it applies to persistence. As we previously noted, students who understand that their performance is linked to their efforts, rather than innate talent, are more resilient and achieve at higher levels. The feedback we provide students should expand their understanding of how they affect their own learning. When we say to a student, "Your comments in that discussion helped everyone understand this idea," we are giving her feedback about the importance of her participation in the classroom. Sometimes this type of feedback may be more behavioral in nature, as when Doug rested his hand on the shoulder of a student who had distanced himself from his lab group and quietly said, "When you moved your chair back from the table, you stopped learning about the interaction of those two compounds. When you're part of the group, you and your lab partners learn together." The ability to help ourselves is an important life skill, and one with which some students struggle. We want students to see how their actions positively affect their own learning.

Feedback About the Self as a Person. This type of feedback is less effective than the others because it often gives the learner little information that can be put to use. Often described as general praise, feedback about the self as a person can include statements like, "Great job!" or "Nice going!" We should always encourage our students, but vague, nonspecific statements like these have little or no effect on motivation, engagement, or learning. More specific feedback related to the task, process, or self-regulation can be more effective. For instance, telling a student, "You attended three tutorials this week, and it really paid off on your test results. I admire your determination," allows the student to translate the feedback into advice on how to further self-regulate.

The research about feedback is complex, but it can be summarized in several key points. First, feedback is most useful when it is accompanied by direction for a further task, such as cueing the student on where to find the error *and* what he can do to correct it. Second, the effectiveness of the feedback decreases when it is focused solely on ability, but strengthened when it is focused on effort, as this has a positive effect on self-regulation. Finally, feedback should not be confused with praise, which can also play a positive role but does not provide the student with information about learning.

Criteria for Feedback

There's nothing more frustrating than laboring over a paper, only to get nothing more than some vague remarks and a score. How many of us have gotten back an essay with a few marks on it in red pen, some random sentences underlined, *awk* in the margin (we later learned this meant *awkward*), and a grade at the bottom? According to Wiggins (1998), effective feedback is (1) timely, (2) specific, (3) understandable to the learner, and (4) actionable.

Timeliness. The timing of feedback has a direct relationship to the learning that occurs. Of course, it should not be so late that the assignment is all but forgotten—feedback on an essay written six weeks earlier isn't of much benefit. What is less commonly known is that feedback should be offered judiciously based on where the student is in the learning cycle. As we noted in the previous section, feedback is at its most effective when the skill or concept being learned is new. This makes a great case for feedback opportunities that are formative, rather than summative.

Tenth grade English teacher Heather Anderson uses a simple checklist (see Figure 6.3) for her students to use in advance of the writing conferences she holds with them. "This checklist shifts the conversation from strictly one which is a 'read and assess,' to one where they are taking a lead on how their essay is taking shape," she told us. "It also lets me move away from focusing on those low-level things like conventions so that we can use the conference time to concentrate on more complex ideas, such as argumentation, claims, and warrants."

Ms. Anderson finds that holding weekly conferences with students is more useful than simply giving students a grade after the essay has been turned in. "Really, that's too late for them," she said. "How could they do anything with feedback at that point? The grade should almost be an afterthought. By the time they're ready to turn in their work, they should be able to predict the grade themselves."

Specificity. Vague feedback isn't especially useful to anyone, let alone students attempting to master new content. In fact, lack of specificity can result in the student interpreting the feedback as negative. When a teacher says, "That's nice," with no other information, the student might internally wonder whether she

Figure 6.3

Sample Writing Conference Checklist

English Period: _____

Checklist/Scoring Rubric for Essential Essay Question #2: Can You Buy Your Way to Happiness?

_____ My essay addresses the essential question: Can you buy your way to happiness? (3 points)

_____ My essay has a minimum of five paragraphs. (5 points)
_____ Introduction/Hook paragraph
_____ Minimum of three body paragraphs
_____ Closing statement/Summary paragraph

_____ My essay is properly formatted. (16 points)
_____ Main text is Times New Roman type, size 12, double spaced
_____ Top right corner has my name, date, English period (single spaced)
_____ Title is centered at the beginning of the essay
_____ Each paragraph is indented

_____ My essay properly cites a minimum of two different sources. (10 points)

_____ My essay has a "works cited" page. (5 points)

_____ My essay uses correct spelling and avoids common errors. It makes sense and addresses the question at all times. (20 points)

_____ A minimum of three people, including myself, proofread and edited my rough draft. Think about whether or not it makes sense, answers the essential question and uses correct spelling and punctuation! (6 points)

Signatures

_____ Myself (2 points)

_____ A peer (2 points)

_____ An adult (2 points)

_____ My edited rough drafts were turned in with my final draft. **(You MUST show that they were all edited by being written on.)** (5 points)

_____ My final draft, rough draft(s), and checklist were turned in by 3:30, Tuesday, December 15. (5 points) did something wrong or is somehow lacking in ability, or sus-pect that the teacher has a lower expectation for her as an individual (Shute, 2008). Specific feedback, meanwhile, gives the student direction for what to do next.

When 2nd grade teacher Roberto Rodriguez meets with small groups for guided reading instruction, he keeps specificity of feedback in mind. For example, when a student was struggling with prosody in oral reading, he said to her, "When you see the quotation marks, that's a reminder to make it sound like talking. Let's try that again." Another student had difficulty reading the word *calendar* in a sentence. "You're having trouble with that word, aren't you?" said Mr. Rodriguez. "Try chunking the word and saying each syllable out loud. That way you can hear it, and I'll bet you'll recognize it."

After the lesson, we talked with Mr. Rodriguez. "I'm working on being more specific about the feedback I give students so that they can key in on the error and resolve it," he said. "It's harder for me, because it would be a lot easier to just give them the answer. It's pushing me to figure out how to be specific, and how to tie it to the next step they should take to solve it."

Actionability. Mr. Rodriguez's comment leads directly to a third condition of effective feedback: that it should be actionable. Simply providing correction isn't adequate; feedback should suggest what steps to take next. By giving students direction, teachers help students understand that errors are not perma-nent and that they possess the ability to fix them. Examples of actionable feedback include the following:

1. Reread that last passage to find the information your answer is missing.

2. Try reading aloud the paragraph that you just wrote, so you can hear what it sounds like.

3. The problem is correct up until this step, but you're introducing a calculation error when you factor the variables. Check your arithmetic again, and I think you'll find the mistake.

Although the content of each of these examples is varied, they all have one thing in common: they don't provide the answers, but they give the learner feedback about what to do *next*. Importantly, they don't overwhelm the learner with larger tasks that leave her wondering where to begin. Telling a student, "The answers to the last three problems are wrong—try it again" leaves the learner with a job that may be too large for her to take on. Some error analysis and a direction for the next action to take can create the cognitive momentum that a learner might need to take on longer and more complex tasks.

Understandability. Feedback should match the developmental, language, and cognitive needs of the student. For example, it can be helpful for English language learners to get feedback in both written and oral forms so that their linguistic memory isn't taxed more than need be.

Rubrics and checklists like the one Ms. Anderson used on her English essay assignment are helpful in making the feedback understandable, but so are simpler practices, like the one Brian Eastman uses in his 7th grade social studies classes. Many of Mr. Eastman's students are English language learners, so he is cognizant of the need to use multiple modalities when providing feedback. "All my students have a 'To Do' section in their notebooks," he said. "I have them section off the last 20 pages when we're setting up the notebooks at the beginning of the year. Whenever I meet with them—even when it's just stopping by their desk—I have them open up the 'To Do' section. As I'm giving them feedback, I also make a list for them of what we're talking about. I date it, so they don't get it confused with other conversations."

Feedback on the Critter Project

Earlier in this chapter we described the project that Mr. Bonine designed for his Biology students to learn about the biological and environmental factors that influence an organism's development. Because Mr. Bonine knows that his feedback is critical to ensuring successful learning outcomes, he makes sure to meet at least twice each class period with each group. He knows that the feedback he provides should be timely, specific, actionable, and understandable. When he meets with one group, he says, "I can see that you've got the basic environmental information for your critter listed here. As I'm reading, I can see you've got information on the dietary and habitat needs of it. But now I'm wondering: What are the shelter needs? You listed predators, but I'm not sure how your critter is going to protect itself. Talk about that with each other, and I'll check back with you in about 10 minutes. It seems your group comes up with great ideas when you put your heads together."

In this example, Mr. Bonine's feedback is focused on both the task and the process. In addition, he has refrained from feedback at the personal level, instead providing self-regulatory information about the usefulness of the students' discussions.

Conclusion

As students engage in tasks, assignments, and activities, they should be provided with opportunities to interact with their peers, their teachers, and the curriculum. This interaction ensures that students develop sophisticated understandings of the content, because they can work in the zone of proximal development. Meaningful tasks also allow students opportunities to use academic English and engage in argumentation, both of which are necessary for success in college and careers.

When students engage in meaningful tasks and receive appropriate feedback about their performance, they can't help but learn. We are reminded of a quote from Marshall McLuhan, the Canadian philosopher: "Everybody experiences far more than he understands. Yet it is experience, rather than understanding, that influences behavior." As teachers, we aim for understanding, yet we know that every experience we provide our students affects their behavior. That's why we have to ensure that their experiences are meaningful.

7

Knowing When a Learning Target Has Been Met

As teachers, we need ways to determine when learning targets have been met. When we have a clear purpose for each lesson, we can identify the ways that students can demonstrate their understanding. A lack of purpose makes it very hard to figure out what kind of evidence we want to see. In this chapter, we focus on some of the many ways that students can demonstrate their mastery of content. We have organized this chapter into sections devoted to teacher assessment, peer assessment, and student self-assessment.

Teacher Assessments

There are a number of ways that teachers can assess student performance, both summatively and formatively. The key is to ensure that the assessments align with the purpose of the lesson. For example, assessing students using a multiple-choice test works in some situations and doesn't work well in others.

It's not that multiple-choice tests are good or bad, but rather that they need to adequately provide teachers with information about whether a learning target has been met. Teachers can assess student learning through nonwritten as well as written modalities. We'll examine both types of assessment below.

Nonwritten Assessments

One of the most common ways to determine whether students have met the purpose of a lesson is through the use of verbal or other nonwritten assessments. We pose questions, engage students in discussion, ask them to explain their thinking, and have them justify their expressed opinions. Some of these practices are accomplished at the individual level, especially when we get a chance to confer with a single student. More often, we have to rely on feedback from a large group of students. The following verbal and nonverbal approaches to checking for understanding can provide teachers and students with information about success and needed instruction.

Fist to Five. This approach is useful for checking in with the entire class at the same time. When the teacher asks a question, the students raise their hands and respond by displaying a chosen number of fingers. For example, Mr. Adams might say the following to his students: "Have we met the purpose yet? If you are still really confused about the flow of electrons, hold up your fist. If you're just getting the idea of electron flow, hold up one finger. If you totally get this and are ready to explain this to me or another person in the room, hold up five fingers. And if you're somewhere in between, hold up two, three, four fingers, depending on your level of understanding right now." Looking around the room, Mr. Adams quickly learns that the majority of students are at the four and five level, but three of them are either at zero or one.

Although the fist-to-five approach is really a form of self-assessment and needs to be backed up by other sources, it can let teachers know which students need attention immediately.

Retelling. Retelling is a fairly simple classroom routine in which students verbally share their understanding of some topic or text (Applegate, Quinn, & Applegate, 2004). Typically, the teacher models what a retelling sounds like before asking students to retell on their own. This approach is most often used with individual students, but works with groups of students as well. Retellings are meant to communicate facts in chronological order, and can be used for a number of different purposes in the classroom. They're easily used in checking for understanding of informational texts. For example, when teacher Shelly McGuire wanted to know if her students understood the information presented in a video about the circulatory system, she asked students to retell information from memory. Ms. McGuire had given each student several slips of paper with key vocabulary words from the video written on them, then asked the students to sort the words in the order that they were presented in the video. Ms. McGuire used the information gathered from the retellings to determine which students needed additional instruction and which students had met the learning target. Figure 7.1 shows a rubric that teachers can use to assess students' retellings.

Student Think-Alouds. Teachers usually model thinking aloud during the focus lesson. Communicating your thought process verbally is an especially powerful way to dispel students' misconceptions about the nature of thinking. Think-alouds

Figure 7.1

Rubric for Assessing Retelling of Informational Text

Element	Exceeds Standards (3)	Meets Standards (2)	Needs Improvement (1)	Score
Key Ideas	Your retelling identified all of the key ideas from the text.	Your retelling identified a number of key ideas from the text.	Your retelling needs to identify and describe the key ideas from the text.	
Details	Your retelling helps others understand the text by providing details for each key idea.	Your retelling provides some details for some of the key ideas.	Your retelling needs to link details with key ideas.	
Sequence	Your retelling identifies a clear sequence of information that helps the listener understand the information.	Your retelling provides information in a sequence but the sequence was slightly confused or out of order.	Your retelling needs to have a sequence that helps the listener understand.	
Conclusion	Your retelling ends with a conclusion that is directly linked to the information you provided.	Your retelling includes a concluding statement.	Your retelling needs to focus the major idea from the text, and this needs to summarize the information gathered.	
Delivery	You use good rhythm, fluency, expression, and gestures.	Your rhythm and expression were good most of the time and you used some gestures.	Your retelling needs to include expression and gestures.	

are typically in the first-person (e.g., "When I read this last paragraph, I realized for the first time that the boy's description of his journey was really from a dream") and describe the cognitive process that leads the speaker to certain conclusions (e.g., "I know it was a dream because I starting thinking about the locations and realized he couldn't have been to all those places"). We supply lots of sticky notes for students to use when they conduct think-alouds. Sometimes we mark a passage or underline a sentence in a reading and ask the students to write down what they are thinking as they read on the sticky notes, which they then place on a copy of the reading that they return to us. These notes allow us to assess how well students understood the purposes of the lesson.

Questions. Another way that teachers check for understanding is by using questions targeted directly at the lesson's purpose. In Chapter 2, we described the revised Bloom's Taxonomy for the 21st century (Anderson et al., 2001), an excellent means for organizing questions across knowledge domains. For effectively designed questions to yield quality responses, however, teachers need to provide students with adequate wait time in which to respond—typically 5–7 seconds of silence after the question is posed, along with another period of wait time after the student has replied. Teachers sometimes forget this second period of wait time, but it is necessary to prevent inadvertently clipping the student's response. If the question is rich, students will often add more information when given the time to do so. Such extended student responses will furnish more information about the extent to which the student has met the learning purpose.

Two other questioning techniques can further reveal whether a student understands: Question-Answer Relationships (QAR) and Question the Author. The QAR technique was developed by Raphael (1986) as a way to develop students' ability to seek out the proper sources of answers to questions. QAR divides questions and answers into the following types:

- "Right There" questions/answers—the student answers by quoting a phrase directly from the text.
- "Think and Search" questions/answers—the student finds the answer by searching across several paragraphs or pages in the text.
- "Author and You" questions/answers—the student answers using information supplied by the text but also draws on his own life experiences. For instance, asking "Would you make the same decision?" requires students to understand a decision described in a text, but to formulate an opinion of their own.
- "On Your Own" questions/answers—the student's answer is not text-dependent in any way (e.g., "Was there ever a time when you . . .").

Esther Firestone teaches 4th grade students, many of whom are English language learners. From the beginning of the year, she teaches them the QAR framework so they can more deliberately locate the source of their answers. She has found the framework to be especially useful when students are taking tests and other formal assessments. "I try to construct my tests in ways that are similarly formatted to the state assessments," she said. "I will often put a passage on there for them to read and answer questions about. I have an extra blank for them to write the abbreviations for the QAR types. I ask them not only for the answer, but for the source of the answer, too. When I look at their correct or incorrect answers, I get a better idea of where they are looking for the information."

An important shift in the Common Core Standards, discussed in Chapter 2, is the need for students to be able to read closely for analysis and discussion—to comprehend the information as well as the author's message, and in some cases to ground that message within historical, cultural, political, and societal contexts. The Questioning the Author (QtA) strategy devised by Beck, McKeown, Hamilton, and Kucan (1997) invites students to go beyond the literal meaning of a text by staging query points throughout the reading. Beck and colleagues encourage teachers to identify query points in advance of a reading. The following examples are typical of QtA queries:

- What do you believe the author is trying to say?
- The author's making an interesting word choice here. Why do you think she picked that phrase?
- Think about what was happening in the author's country at that time. How do you understand that last paragraph, reading it from a landowner's perspective?

Mindy Le knows that QtA queries require thought, so she plans them in advance of her 8th grade social studies lessons. "I used QtA to assist my students in understanding the Declaration of Independence," she said. "To them it looks like a stuffy, old document. I want them to see it as the act of rebellion it really was." She goes so far as to enlist students to play the roles of some of the Declaration's signers. "I have them assigned as teams for each of the men, and they use the QtA questions I've prepared to question one another." Each team is equipped with a short biography to discuss in advance. One question— "Why did you sign this when you knew you were risking your life?"—brought a heartfelt response from the students representing New Jersey delegate Richard Stockton. One student spoke on her team's behalf: "I have been a lawyer and a judge, and I always hoped we could work out our problems with England. But we can't. The Stamp Act proved that to me. I want to be the first one to sign from my colony." By supplying biographical information for students to understand the lives of the signers, Ms. Le was able to ensure that her students gained a deeper appreciation for the landmark document.

Written Assessments

Written assessments are a staple of any classroom, and with good reason: The permanent nature of writing makes it possible for the teacher to examine evidence of student learning more thoroughly, whereas the transience of the spoken word is difficult to recall after a busy day of teaching. However, extended writing presents its own unique problems, especially for secondary teachers who have student rosters of 150 or more a day. As we noted in Chapter 6, effective feedback needs to be timely if it is to be useful. One way to address this issue is to use any of the following short writing routines, keeping in mind that their purpose is to ascertain whether students grasped the purpose of the day's lesson.

Caption Writing. Ninth-grade Earth science teacher Adam Renick is an outdoor adventurer in his spare time, and tries to bring the world into his classroom whenever possible. He travels extensively during school breaks to remote outposts and photographs his surroundings for use in his classroom. On a day when his purpose was to introduce the concept of weathering and erosion, he prepared a video slide show of photographs he had taken of geological formations. He showed the slide show to his students while explaining what the formations were, where they were located, and how they were formed. Before replaying the slide show, he explained that he would stop the video periodically so that the students could caption some of the slides using the terminology he had introduced earlier in the lesson. Each time Mr. Renick stopped the slide show, his students worked at their table groups to discuss possible captions and then log them in their science notebooks. After class, Mr. Renick reviewed the captions to see how well his students grasped the new vocabulary and whether they accurately described the formations.

Summarizing. The ability to write accurate summaries is arguably the most useful kind of academic writing. In every content area, students are required to digest a large volume of information and then streamline it to describe what's most important. Written summaries are an excellent method for discovering what students have taken away from the day's lesson. These can take the form of "exit slips" that students hand in just before leaving the classroom or shifting to the next content area. World history teacher Jo Schaefer uses exit slips several times a week to discover which students have met the lesson's purpose and which would benefit from further instruction. The content purpose of one lesson was to examine the role of the influenza pandemic of 1918–19 in bringing World War I to an end, and the language purpose was for students to use the notes to justify their opinions. After examining primary source documents from the era and listening to presentations from virologists and historians, the students discussed what they learned in small groups. As a final step, they wrote short exit slips answering the question, "Did influenza bring an end to the Great War?" Ahmed wrote the following (spelling and grammar errors included):

> In my opinion, the influenza pandemic was like the straw that broke the camel's back. In Germany the Kaiser was already having trouble with feeding the people, and their

was lots of people who were starving to death. Then the United States joined the war and that was like a phsychologocal boost because they were all fresh and strong. The bad thing was that the influenza snuck up on everyone in the world. It was like it was all good in 1918, and then people got sick really fast. This influenza strane was bad too because it killed people between 15–34 the most and that was the age of the soldiers in the armies. I think when Germany surrendered in 1918 it was like the influenza forced them to get out of a war that was too bad for the German people to endure.

Ms. Schaefer read the exit slips quickly in between classes to get a sense of what students had learned or still had misconceptions about, allowing her to make adjustments for the next period and revisit concepts the following day. Later, she scored the slips using the rubric in Figure 7.2. She noted minor problems with conventions in Ahmed's summary, and was pleased to see that his sentence variety was increasing. She was most pleased to see that he used academic vocabulary accurately and to good effect, even using the term "psychological boost," which she had discussed in a previous lesson. Most important, Ahmed was synthesizing information across several lessons, and his summary sentence at the beginning of the exit slip displayed creativity. This summary let her know that Ahmed was on track to learning about a complex time in history.

Generative Sentences. In every content area, students must master the vocabulary of the discipline. But teaching isolated words is ineffective; the artificial nature of a word list fails to mimic the way the vocabulary is really used. Students need to use vocabulary to express ideas, as the vocabulary is really a proxy for the concepts it represents. One way to move from

Figure 7.2
Summary Rubric

	Exceeds the Standard (4)	Meets the Standard (3)	Approaches the Standard (2)	Not at Standard (1)
Conventions and Mechanics	• Mastery of grammar, usage, mechanics, and spelling • Diverse sentence starters and varied sentence structure	• Control of usage, grammar, mechanics, and spelling • Different sentence starters with some attempts at sentence variety	• Some intrusive errors in grammar, usage, mechanics, and spelling • Little sentence variety in terms of starters, length, or type	• Many serious and intrusive errors in grammar, usage, mechanics, and spelling • Formulaic and constrained sentences
Academic Vocabulary	• Consistent use of technical vocabulary • Correct use of specialized, multiple-meaning words	• Consistent use of technical vocabulary • Incorrect use of specialized words	• Weak use of technical vocabulary • Incorrect use of specialized words	• No use of technical vocabulary • Incorrect use of specialized words
Content	• Insightful summarizing sentence • Highlighting of all key points and omission of unnecessary details	• Clear summarizing sentence • Highlighting of most key points and omission of most unnecessary details	• Summarizing sentence attempted • Highlighting of several key points but inclusion of unnecessary details	• No summarizing sentence • No highlighting of necessary key points and inclusion of several unnecessary details

definitional instruction, which is necessary but not sufficient, to expression, is to use generative sentences. Students write sentences using targeted vocabulary following conditions about length and word position. Here are some examples of teacher instructions for writing generative sentences:

- Write a sentence of at least six words that has the word *pet* in the second position.
- Write a sentence that has the word *geography* in the third position.
- Write a sentence of at least nine words that begins with the word *although*.
- Write a sentence with the term *algorithm* in a sentence between 10 and 12 words in length.

As you can see from these examples, conditions can be made more or less difficult depending on the needs of the learners. This writing activity takes only a few minutes, but gets students putting ideas down on paper. These sentences can then form an opening or topic sentence for a paragraph.

First grade teacher Daya Mehta provides even more scaffolded support for her students when they create generative sentences. She begins by asking students to think of a word that has the letter V in the third position. "Think of your word and then write it down," she says. She then asks the children to share their words with the class. "Love," one girl says. "Have," says another. "Give," offers a third. "Those are great examples," remarks Ms. Mehta. "Now take one of those words and make a sentence that starts with it." After the students spend two or three minutes writing a sentence, Ms. Mehta asks for more examples. "Hives have bees," Ryan says. "Move out of the way!" says Monica. They repeat the task with several other letters, until each student has written four sentences. "Now I'd like for you to choose your favorite sentence and use it in a paragraph that's at least three sentences long," says Ms. Mehta. "I can't wait to read what you write about!" In 10 minutes, Ms. Mehta has moved her students from letter level to word level, then sentence level, and now paragraph level. "I can get a handle on where each student is having difficulty when we use generative sentences," she said later. "If there's a breakdown somewhere, I can see precisely where it is."

Tests. Although tests are frequently thought of strictly as summative assessments, they can and should be used for formative assessment as well. Short quizzes that are low-risk provide both the teacher and the student with feedback about what is known and not known at a given moment in time. The key, of course, is to truly make them low-risk; surprise quizzes are likely to cause more stress and may have a negative effect on the learning environment.

Using different test constructs in low-risk assignments and quizzes can be quite useful, especially if they are used to draw conclusions about learning and inform practice. The most commonly used formats are multiple choice and short answer. Multiple-choice tests limit learners to responses that have been designed in advance. One advantage to this type of test lies in the design of the "distracters"—that is, the incorrect items in the set of possible answers. Good distracters should serve a diagnostic purpose, and thus should be more or less plausible answers to the given question.

Kitt Holloway, a 6th grade physical science teacher, anticipates that her students will have misconceptions about the universe at the beginning of an astronomy unit. Moreover, she knows that these misconceptions are difficult to dislodge. Several times a week, she has her students complete a short multiple-choice quiz featuring distracters that suggest that stars stay in the same place night after night, that the galaxy is crowded, and that the brightness of a star or planet is related only to its distance from the Earth. "I get great feedback on the students' progress as I'm teaching," she said. "Even though I'm clear about the purpose, some of these ideas about the way the physical world functions are firmly in place." Ms. Holloway uses an audience-response system rather than paper and pencil, so that students can see how everyone is answering. "I post the question and have the students respond, and they get to see the percentage who chose each item. I don't tell them the answer, but I ask them to explain their choice to their partner," she said. "Then I post the question again, and they respond again. It's amazing to see the shift to the correct answer, before I've even told them." Ms. Holloway follows the second round of responses with more instruction, if needed. "If lots of students are still not solid, I know to reteach," she said. "But I also know when I don't need to reteach."

Short-answer tests are common at every level, from the primary grades on. Students provide written responses to questions, and their answers vary from a few words to a few sentences in length. Short-answer tests can be a bit more challenging than multiple-choice tests as they require recall of information, rather than recognition. As a rule, short-answer items are written as complete questions rather than as partial statements followed by a blank that the student must complete. Fill-in-the-blank questions can be confusing for some English learners and students with language disabilities.

Doug recalls a particularly revealing use of short-answer questions in a 2nd grade class that he taught. Nico, a 2nd grader, had just read a humorous story about Humpty Dumpty filing a lawsuit after falling off the wall. When he finished, Nico turned his attention to the short-answer comprehension questions at the end of the text. One question read, "Who is Humpty Dumpty suing?" Nico wrote, "Humpty Dumpty is an egg." Seeing the error, Doug asked Nico about it. It turns out that Nico didn't know the word *suing*, so he simply ignored it. To Nico, the question became, "Who is Humpty Dumpty?" In the story, the words *sue* and *sues* were used, but not the word *suing*, so Nico didn't recognize it. This was a great reminder that incorrect answers are rarely random; the answer that students furnish is based on what they know and do not know *at that time*. Our job as teachers is to figure out what that might be, so we know how to respond next in our teaching.

Peer Assessments

Mention *peer assessments* and many teachers will have a moment of discomfort, perhaps spurred by a memory of their own schooling. Nancy remembers attending 1st grade at an overcrowded elementary school where she and 49 other six-year-olds learned how to read, add, and do the other things most 1st graders do. At the time, it didn't seem alarming that there was a single teacher for all these little children, although the thought causes her to shudder now. As you can imagine, the number of students made it difficult to get much done, so the teacher had them regularly checking and grading each other's papers. This was in the days of endless worksheets (no wonder, with 50 students in the class), so there were a lot of papers to grade. Five or six times a day, children traded papers, and the teacher read the correct answers. The students dutifully marked each with a check or an "X," then tallied the score at the top. You could only hope that the person who got your paper was paying attention and didn't mark a correct answer as being wrong. The teacher certainly wasn't going to recheck it. Is this what we mean by peer assessment?

In a word, no. The intention of Nancy's overworked teacher was to save a bit of time grading an endless stream of worksheets. The teacher didn't attempt to use other sources of information to see how well students were understanding material, and the assessments were summative only, never formative. According to Topping (2008), *formative* peer assessment helps students "plan their learning, identify their strengths and weaknesses, target areas for remedial action, and develop metacognitive and other personal and professional skills" (p. 20). In other words, peer assessments are reciprocal—they provide both the assessor and the assessed with information that they can apply to their own learning. But peer assessment does require careful planning and instruction to be properly implemented, and so that students understand the benefits.

Although the evidence shows that the efforts of trained peer assessors are reliable and valid when compared to their teachers' efforts, students often prefer the teacher's assessment over those completed by peers (Weaver, 1995). For this reason, it is helpful to situate the peer-assessment process within the overall context of the development of the project or assignment. This approach can alleviate students' concerns about whether the feedback they are getting from their peers is useful. In addition, it is good practice for the teacher to be an active participant in the formative assessment process. Otherwise, students may perceive that they are doing "your" work and may resent having to participate.

Roundtable Peer Assessments

Chen (2010) describes the following model of peer assessment, called the Mobile Assessment Participation System (MAPS), that relies on active teacher participation throughout:

1. The teacher and students discuss and co-select the assessment criteria or scoring rubrics.
2. Roundtable formats help students conduct the presentation, give and receive feedback, and conduct peer- and self-assessments.
3. Students reflect on feedback from the teacher or peers and revise their performance.
4. If needed, the peer assessment cycle is repeated (steps 1–3).
5. Students submit their final work. (p. 231)

The roundtable format lies at the heart of this approach. Students work in self-selected small groups based on a topic of interest. Each student presents his or her project or assignment, fielding questions from the others. Using a rubric or other assessment criteria, the peers score the assignment and give the score to the presenter, who has also scored himself or herself. The presenter is asked to reflect on any discrepancies between the self-assessment and the one received from peers and revise as necessary. This process can be repeated as needed. The teacher has an active role throughout, moving from group to group during the roundtable discussions and conferring with students individually after they have reflected on the feedback from peers.

Sixth grade teacher Mary Ellen Thomas uses the roundtable process during the weeks leading up to her school's science fair.

Because the projects for the fair are complex and often require weeks of preparation, her students have difficulty seeing them through in a meaningful way. "In the past, I saw a fair number of students who just wanted to get something—anything, really—done," said Ms. Thomas. "The learning, the inquiry weren't there. That's why I started doing Science Roundtable once a week." She divides the roundtables into several categories—life sciences, physical sciences, psychological sciences, and Earth sciences—and has students select the group that best describes their own project. Each week, the roundtable members discuss the status of their projects, asking questions of one another and making suggestions. They use a rubric developed by Ms. Thomas for the science fair, as well as a checklist that details where they should be in the process. Students score the description of the project thus far and give it to the presenter, and the presenter self-assesses. The next day Ms. Thomas meets individually with each student to discuss the peer- and self-assessments. "It keeps them on track, and holds them accountable to each other," she said. "After all, scientists talk to each other about their projects, so I want my students to do so as well."

Written Peer Responses

Some prefer the term *peer response* to *peer assessment*, as it better emphasizes the formative, rather than evaluative, nature of the process. Simmons (2003) worked with four high school English classes to examine the qualities of effective peer response, and the ways in which they can be taught. He described four types of peer response that were common but not helpful: *global praise*, which provides validation but not much more; *personal response*, which spotlights the reader's own personal experiences; and *sentence edits* and *word edits*, which focus on conventions. Three other types of peer response were of greater value:

- *Text playback*, which centers on the structure of the paper (e.g., "The thesis statement at the beginning gave me a clear idea of where you were going with this.");
- *Reader's needs*, which provides the writer with feedback from an audience (e.g., "I got confused when these two characters were arguing. Who was the one who hit the wall with his fist?"); and
- *Writer's strategies*, which focuses on techniques for expression of ideas (e.g., "You could label each section with a heading.").

Knowing what is effective and ineffective when it comes to peer response is one thing; teaching these behaviors to students is another. Simmons (2003) recommends lots of teacher modeling to promote effective peer response, as this allows students to witness the expert thinking of their teacher as well as the specific behaviors that they should be using. A chart summarizing modeling strategies for different elements of peer response can be found in Figure 7.3.

Peer Assessments in Digital Environments

The increased use of digital learning environments has provided a new platform for peer assessment and response. Because the field is so new, there is not much research on effective practices. However, the anecdotal information we have offers both potential and caution about its use. On the one hand, a classroom wiki offers new possibilities for students to create together, especially in collaborating on projects and

Figure 7.3

Techniques to Teach Peer Responding

Technique	What the Teacher Does	What Students Do
Sharing your writing	Shares a piece of writing and asks for response Shares rewrites tied to class response	Offers comments on the teacher's writing
Clarifying evaluation vs. response	Shows evaluation is of product, while response is to writer	Understand that response is personable and helpful
Modeling specific praise	Shows how to tell what you like as a reader	Understand that cheerleading is too general to be helpful
Modeling understanding	Shows how to tell what you understood the piece to be about	Understand that reflecting back the piece to the writer is helpful
Modeling questions	Shows how to ask questions about what you didn't understand	Understand that questions related to the writer's purpose are helpful
Modeling suggestions	Shows how to suggest writing techniques	Understand that a responder leaves the writer knowing what to do next
Whole-class response	Moderates response by class to one classmate's piece	Offer response Hear the response of others Hear what the writer finds helpful
Partner response	Pairs up students in class to respond to pieces	Practice response learned in whole-class session
Comment review	Reads the comments of peers to writers Suggests better techniques Devises focus lessons	Get teacher feedback on comments
Response conference	Speaks individually with students responding inappropriately	Have techniques reinforced

Source: From "Responders Are Taught, Not Born," by J. Simmons, 2003, *Journal of Adolescent and Adult Literacy, 46*(8), p. 690. Reprinted with permission of the International Reading Association.

assignments. Students can easily share and view work with one another, and feedback and peer responses are not limited by the bell-to-bell nature of the school day. On the other hand, there can be a difference in the interaction styles of two students when they are not seated physically close to one another. The distance afforded by a digital environment can make it easy to engage in other, distracting activities, diluting the quality of the interaction. We would never dream of checking our email when someone was in a conversation with us, but a digital environment makes it easier to do so. In addition, the ability to post anonymous feedback has the potential to devolve into mean-spirited or insensitive comments that are not constructive.

As with face-to-face peer response opportunities, peer assessments in digital environments are best supported by instruction on the process, along with rubrics or other tools that can facilitate the use of helpful feedback. In addition, it can be helpful to create a process for allowing authors to provide feedback to the peer reviewer about the usefulness of the comments. Such reciprocity encourages more dialogue, rather than one-way communication. Features vary across platforms, but most have some kind of discussion capacity, and some may even allow for real-time chats.

Peer assessments and dialogue can be especially critical during extended collaborative group projects conducted in an online environment. Most of us have experienced unsuccessful group-work experiences, and the problems are predictable. Jalajas and Sutton (1985) studied feuds in student groups and identified five negative roles: (1) the whiner, who complains a lot; (2) the martyr, who volunteers for more work but lets everyone know what a burden it is; (3) the bully, whose

interactions intimidate others; (4) the deadbeat, who does little work; and (5) the saboteur, who undermines the group by
making changes without consulting others. Concerned about
the damaging impact of these behaviors in an online environment, Brandyberry and Bakke (2006) added a simple activity
log module that group members could use to record their daily
contributions and the amount of time spent on the activity.
Other members of the group could view these entries as well,
making it possible for all to monitor the efforts of each other in
a formative way, and provide each other feedback. The authors
found this approach to be far more constructive than the more
conventional process of rating each other's efforts at the end
of the project.

Todd Mendenhall, an 11th grade U.S. history teacher, has
found that using an interactive digital log gives collaborative
groups much more insight about themselves and their peers.
His class created multimedia projects comparing the use of
persuasion and propaganda by Nazi Germany and the United
States during World War II to increase domestic support for the
war effort. Although students met regularly in class, these times
were brief and were mostly for status checks and planning. The
majority of their work was outside of class, and in past years this
arrangement fostered resentment in some groups. "You know, if
they're not seeing each other work, they tend to think they're
the only ones putting in the hours," the teacher said. Using his
district's e-platform, he created a page where group members
logged in how they spent their time and how much time they
devoted to the project. Group members are also required to
comment on each other's project log each week.

"It's the first year I've done this," said Mr. Mendenhall, "but I
can already hear the tone of the conversations changing. The

groups are spending less time on trying to figure out where they're at, because they can see and comment on the logs. It's helpful for me, too, because if I see a problem emerging I can respond more quickly. I pulled aside one student last week because he wasn't pulling his weight. By my talking with him about it, it wasn't up to the group alone to manage this problem. I'm happy to say that the log he entered this week is much more in line with the others. The peer assessments I'm reading are improved, too. Instead of focusing on character qualities, the comments are mostly about the content and the task. Much more focused."

Student Self-Assessment

A major purpose of having peer assessments is to increase learners' ability to assess themselves. Mr. Mendenhall's use of interactive digital project logs is designed in part to give students feedback from their peers so they can revise and adjust. The ability to notice when one has learned something and when something remains unclear is vital for academic success. Young children in particular often find this skill difficult to master, due in large part to developmental factors that limit their language ability. Although primary students have an explosion of vocabulary growth during their first years of school, they do not typically have the vocabulary to express what is going on in their own minds. A 2nd grader isn't likely to say, "You know, I've been noticing that my attention wanders during math when the processes get confusing. Could you slow down and write each step in a different color so I can see it?" Instead, we're left to witness the outward behavior of a daydreamer looking out the window during math. It is therefore helpful to provide students with concrete ways to reflect on their learning through classroom processes that build their self-assessment vocabulary, such as goal-setting sheets, K-W-L charts, and I-Search papers.

Goal-Setting Sheets. The students in Velma Johnson's 2nd grade classroom set academic goals for themselves each morning and assess their progress at the end of the day. They begin with a learning goal for the day, using statements that Ms. Johnson has displayed for them all around the room. She models how she sets her own learning goals, thinking aloud as she writes them. The focus of the goals change: one day they may be oriented toward reading and writing, while on other days they may be about math, asking for and offering help, or even getting along with others in the class. About 10 minutes before the end of the school day, her students pull their goal-setting sheets out and rate their own progress. These self-ratings are a ticket out the door—Ms. Johnson stands by the door collecting them and saying good-bye to each student. "It gives me a way to check in with each student," she said. "I can read the goals they have for themselves and what they think of their efforts. I start to notice patterns, like with Deon, who is quiet in class. I've discovered from his goal sheets that he's really hard on himself when he doesn't get a task completed. I talk about the difference between completing a job and learning something, and they're not always the same thing. Sometimes I revisit the purpose statements I use in the lesson with Deon, pointing out to him the learning part." (See Figure 7.4 for an example of a goal-setting sheet for use with younger students.)

K-W-L Charts. This process, first developed by Ogle (1986), has proven popular and enduring because it fosters inquiry, self-reflection, and metacognitive awareness. The K-W-L chart has three columns labeled K, W, and L. Students are asked to list what they know about a topic (K) and what they want

Figure 7.4

Goal-Setting Sheet for Use with Younger Students

My learning goal in reading for today is:

I will know I have met it when:

How did I do?

My learning goal in writing today is:

I will know I have met it when:

How did I do?

to know about it (W). At the end of the period of study on the topic, they return again to the chart and list what they have learned (L). Ogle developed this classroom routine for elementary students, but it has proven to be equally successful for secondary students as well. In fact, an iteration of the strategy called KWL Plus is especially designed for use with older students (Carr & Ogle, 1987). The first three steps are the same, but the "plus" portion emphasizes concept mapping and summarizing. The purpose is for students to organize what they have learned into conceptual categories to deepen their schema about the topic, then use the conceptual map to derive a written summary.

Ninth grade Earth science teacher Adam Renick uses KWL Plus routinely as a way for students to notice their learning when they read in his class. Soon after they began a unit on weathering and erosion, his students read and discussed a reading on the topic. After leading the class through discussion about their background knowledge of weathering, they reviewed photographs of geological formations that Mr. Renick had taken. Students read about the two concepts and listed key ideas as a class. Then, working in pairs, they sorted the facts into coherent categories.

Symone and Kiki created four categories: chemical weathering, physical weathering, erosion, and deposition (a term they encountered in the reading). Mr. Renick also requires students to pose a question about something that is still confusing to them. Symone wrote, "It said that deposition is influenced by velocity. Is that the same as speed?" Kiki wrote, "So is acid precipitation an example of mechanical *and* chemical weathering?" Mr. Renick used the students' summaries as exit slips, collecting them to use for planning the next lesson. "I get a good idea of what students have noticed about their learning through these short summaries," he said. "The day after we do this, I start with reading their questions so we can talk about them. A lot of times there's more than one student who's got a similar question."

I-Search Papers. Middle school students are often required to write research papers on various topics for their classes, and they grow in length and complexity as they advance through high school. These papers often follow a prescriptive format, and the final product reflects what the students have learned about the subject. However, the process of inquiry used to build the paper is often lost in the typically third-person/past-tense voice of the essay. Macrorie (1988) developed an alternative to the traditional research paper, the I-Search, in an attempt to preserve the process of inquiry; as he put it, the student "conducts a search to find out something he needs to know for his own life and writes the story of his adventure" (p. iii). I-Search papers are written in the first person, making them somewhat easier for novice writers because the more formal academic tone is not required.

Many of the elements of an I-Search paper mirror the processes used in K-W-L charts. After selecting a topic (an important first step), the student writes about what he or she already knows and crafts questions meant to guide the search for information. In the body of the paper, the student describes how he can answer these questions using information he has learned, and concludes with new questions that spring from what he has discovered. (Figure 7.5 shows an example of an I-Search paper from English teacher and author Jason Luther.)

Fifth grade teacher Jesse Rimbaud uses a shorter version of the I-Search paper with his students as they investigate the impact of immigration and western movement in the United States. They select a fictional child from the 18th, 19th, or 20th centuries and develop a story of what that person's experiences might have been like.

"I was inspired by baseball cards," Mr. Rimbaud said. "There would be lots of information about players' careers on the back, but the information only hinted at what their experiences might have been. I made similar cards on kids from different

Figure 7.5
Sample I-Search Paper Format

Introduction

1. Describing a genuine problem or situation in life (1–2 pages)
2. Asking a question (or several questions) in response to the problem or situation (1 paragraph)

Body

3. Trying to answer the question by reflecting on personal experience and memory (2 pages)
4. Trying to answer the question by gathering four or five sources from the immediate community and from the library (4–5 pages)
   • Explaining why each source is appropriate
   • Quoting or paraphrasing each source
   • Reflecting on the answers each source gave

Conclusion

5. Concluding by looking back and forward, asking "what did I just learn?" and "what will I do next?" (1 page)

Source: From "I-Searching in Context: Thinking Critically about the Research Unit," by J. Luther, 2006, *English Journal, 95*(4), p. 73. Used with permission.

eras, and challenged my students to create a story." Mr. Rimbaud has cards representing a girl who came to the United States from Ireland in 1790, a boy who traveled on the Oregon Trail, and a Cherokee child on the Trail of Tears.

One card is about a girl named Mardea, who was kidnapped from her village on the Ivory Coast and sold into slavery. Destiny selected her for her I-Search paper, and created a history that chronicled her journey on a slave ship, being sold on an auction block in South Carolina, and her life on a plantation. "The first thing I asked myself was what it would be like to be on a slave ship," said Destiny. "One of the books I read was called *The Middle Passage* (Feelings, 1995), and the pictures really made me shiver. I knew it was awful, but that book got my imagination going." Destiny wrote about the girl's name change to Mary, writing the following on her card:

> Mardea's new master called her Mary. The man couldn't say her name right and probably didn't even try. This was confusing for Mardea. She didn't know anything about the Bible or Christians so the name was weird and didn't belong to her. Even when she was an old woman of 92 and she wasn't a slave anymore because she got freed, Mary said the name she had before got left behind in Africa.

Destiny also wrote about the new questions she had formed because of the project. "I want to learn more about what people like Mardea did after there was no more slavery," she said. "Like, where would you go? Could you find other people in your family or your old friends? I know the Civil War was over but I'd like to know more about what it was like right after, especially when people like her weren't allowed to learn to read or write."

Conclusion

The ultimate reason for establishing a clear purpose is to determine when students have met the learning target and which students still need additional instruction. Purpose is the driving force of a quality lesson plan, and guides teachers and students as they interact with one another in the learning environment. Without purpose, lessons become merely a series of activities or tasks, and students fail to synthesize and consolidate the wonderful experiences they have into a meaningful whole. As we have said before, the short time it takes to establish purpose—perhaps only 30 seconds or so—pays off in huge dividends. But don't forget, there's a lot of backstage preparation to ensure that the purpose is appropriate for the students. We are reminded of a quote from Napoleon Hill, the writer and philosopher who said, "There is no hope of success for the person who does not have a central purpose, or definite goal at which to aim." Let's take aim and help our students soar!

References

Ainsworth, L. (2003). *Unwrapping the standards: A simple process to make standards manageable*. Englewood, CO: Lead + Learn Press.

Anderson, L. W., Krathwohl, D. L., Airasian, P. W., Cruikshank, K. A., Mayer, R. E., Pintrich, P. R., Raths, J., & Wittrock, M. C. (2001). *A taxonomy for learning, teaching, and assessing: A revision of Bloom's taxonomy of educational objectives* (Abridged ed.). Boston: Allyn & Bacon.

Applegate, M. D., Quinn, K. B., & Applegate, A. (2004). *The critical reading inventory*. Upper Saddle River, NJ: Pearson/Merrill Prentice Hall.

Au, K., & Raphael, T. (2007). Classroom assessment and standards-based change. In J. R. Paratore & R. L. McCormack (Eds.), *Classroom literacy assessment: Making sense of what students know and do* (pp. 306–322). New York: Guilford.

Au, W. (2007). High-stakes testing and curricular control: A qualitative metasynthesis. *Educational Researcher, 36*(5), 258–267.

August, D., & Hakuta, K. (Eds.). (1997). *Improving schooling for language-minority children: A research agenda*. Washington, DC: National Academy Press.

Bailey, A. L., & Butler, F. A. (2002). *An evidentiary framework for operationalizing academic language for broad application to K–12 education: A design document*. Los Angeles, CA: National Center for Research on Evaluation, Standards, and Student Testing (CRESST), University of California.

Baker, S. K., Simmons, D. C., & Kame'enui, E. J. (1998). Vocabulary acquisition: Research bases. In D. C. Simmons & E. J. Kame'enui (Eds.),

What reading research tells us about children with diverse learning needs (pp. 183–218). Mahwah, NJ: Lawrence Erlbaum.

Balzer, W. K., Doherty, M. E., & O'Connor, R., Jr. (1989). Effects of cognitive feedback on performance. *Psychological Bulletin, 106*(3), 410–433.

Barrows, H. S., & Tamblyn, R. M. (1976). An evaluation of problem-based learning in small groups utilizing a simulated patient. *Journal of Medical Education, 51*, 52–54.

Battro, A. M., Fischer, K. W., & Léna, P. J. (2008). *The educated brain: Essays in neuroeducation.* New York: Cambridge University Press.

Beck, I. L., McKeown, M. G., Hamilton, R. L., & Kucan, L. (1997). *Questioning the author: An approach for enhancing student engagement with text.* Newark, DE: International Reading Association.

Bellard, B. R., French, B. F., & Ertmer, P. A. (2009). Validity and problem-based learning research: A review of instruments used to assess intended learning outcomes. *The Interdisciplinary Journal of Problem-based Learning, 3*(1), 59–89.

Billingsley, E. F. (1984). Where are the generalized outcomes? An examination of instructional objectives. *The Journal of the Association for Persons with Severe Handicaps, 9*, 182–192.

Bloom, B. S. (Ed.). (1956). *Taxonomy of educational objectives, the classification of educational goals—Handbook I: Cognitive domain.* New York: McKay.

Brandyberry, A. A., & Bakke, S. A. (2006). Mitigating negative behaviors in student project teams: An information technology solution. *Journal of Information Systems Education, 17*(2), 195–209.

Brown, A. L., & Campione, J. C. (1996). Communities of learning and thinking, or a context by any other name. In P. Woods (Ed.), *Contemporary issues in teaching and learning* (pp. 120–126). New York: Routledge.

Brown, C. (2007). Strategies for making social studies texts more comprehensible for English-language learners. *The Social Studies, 98*(5), 185–188.

Burnett, B. C. (2003). The impact of teacher feedback on student self-talk and self-concept in reading and mathematics. *Journal of Classroom Interaction, 38*(1), 11–16.

California Department of Education. (2000). *History–social science content standards for California public schools, kindergarten through grade twelve.* Sacramento, CA: Author.

Campione, J. C. (1981, April). *Learning, academic achievement, and instruction.* Paper presented at the second annual conference on reading research of the study of reading, New Orleans, LA.

Carlo, M. S., August, D., McLaughlin, B., Snow, C. E., Dressler, C., Lippman, D. N., Lively, T. J., & White, C. E. (2004). Closing the gap: Addressing the vocabulary needs of English-language learners in bilingual and mainstream classrooms. *Reading Research Quarterly, 39*(2), 188–215.

Carnegie Council on Adolescent Development. (1989). *Turning points: Preparing American youth for the 21st century*. New York: Carnegie Corporation.

Carr, E., & Ogle, D. (1987). KWL plus: A strategy for comprehension and summarization. *Journal of Reading, 30*(7), 628–631.

Carrier, K. A. (2005). Supporting science learning through science literacy objectives for English language learners. *Science Activities, 42*(2), 5–11.

Chappuis, S., & Chappuis, J. (2008). The best value in formative assessment. *Educational Leadership, 65*(4), 14–19.

Chen, C. (2010). The implementation and evaluation of a mobile- and peer-assessment system. *Computers & Education, 55*(1), 229–236.

Clancy, M. E., & Hruska, B. L. (2005). Developing language objectives for English language learners in physical education lessons. *Journal of Physical Education, Recreation, and Dance, 76*(4), 30–35.

Costa, A. L. (2001). *Developing minds: A resource book for teaching thinking* (3rd ed.). Alexandria, VA: ASCD.

Coxhead, A. (2000). A new academic word list. *TESOL Quarterly, 34*(2), 213–238.

Darling-Hammond, L. (2004). Standards, accountability, and school reform. *Teachers College Record, 106*(6), 1047–1085.

David, J. L. (2008). Pacing guides. *Educational Leadership, 66*(2), 87–88.

Dewey, J. (1902). *The child and the curriculum*. Chicago: University of Chicago Press.

DuFour, R., DuFour, R., Eaker, R., & Karhanek, G. (2004). *Whatever it takes: How professional learning communities respond when kids don't learn*. Bloomington, IN: Solution Tree Press.

Dweck, C. S. (2006). *Mindset: The new psychology of success*. New York: Random House.

Echevarria, J., Short, D., & Powers, K. (2006). School reform and standards-based education: A model for English language learners. *Journal of Educational Research, 99*(4), 195–210.

Ellis, R., Loewen, S., & Erlam, R. (2006). Implicit and explicit corrective feedback and the acquisition of L2 grammar. *Studies in Second Language Acquisition, 28*(2), 268–339.

Feelings, T. (1995). *The middle passage: White ships/black cargo*. New York: Dial.

Fennimore, T. F., & Tinzmann, M. B. (1990). *What is a thinking curriculum?* [Online]. Retrieved from http://www.ncrel.org/sdrs/areas/rpl_esys/thinking.htm

Fisher, D., & Frey, N. (2008). *Better learning through structured teaching*. Alexandria, VA: ASCD.

Fisher, D., & Frey, N. (2010b). Unpacking the language purpose: Vocabulary, structure, and function. *TESOL Journal, 1*(3), 315–337.

Fraser, B. J., Walberg, H. J., Welch, W. W., & Hattie, J. A. (1987). Synthesis of educational productivity research. *Journal of Educational Research, 11*(2), 145–252.

Frey, N., Fisher, D., & Everlove, S. (2009). *Productive group work: How to engage students, build teamwork, and promote understanding.* Alexandria, VA: ASCD.

Frey, N., Fisher, D., & Gonzalez, A. (2010). *Literacy 2.0: Reading and writing in the 21st century.* Bloomington, IN: Solution Tree.

Frey, N., Fisher, D., & Moore, K. (2005). *Designing responsive curriculum: Planning lessons that work.* Lanham, MD: Rowman & Littlefield.

Gagné, R. M., & Briggs, L. J. (1974). *Principles of instructional design.* New York: Rinehart & Wilson.

Golden, J. (2001). *Reading in the dark: Using film as a tool in the English classroom.* Urbana, IL: NCTE.

Graff, G., & Birkenstein, C. (2006). *They say / I say: The moves that matter in academic writing.* New York: W. W. Norton & Company.

Gronlund, N. E., & Linn, R. L. (1990). *Measurement and evaluation in teaching.* Upper Saddle River, NJ: Prentice Hall.

Gunderson, S., Jones, R., Scanland, K. (2005). *The jobs revolution: Changing how America works.* Chicago, IL: Copywriters Incorporated.

Halliday, M. A. K. (1973). *Explorations in the functions of language.* London: Edward Arnold.

Hattie, J. (2009). *Visible learning: A synthesis of over 800 meta-analyses relating to achievement.* New York: Routledge.

Hattie, J., & Timperley, H. (2007). The power of feedback. *Review of Educational Research, 77,* 81–112.

Haughey, D. (2010). SMART goals [Online]. Retrieved from www.projectsmart.co.uk/smart-goals.html

Herzberg, F. (1959). *The motivation to work.* New York: John Wiley and Sons.

Hmelo-Silver, C. E., Duncan, R. G., & Chinn, C. A. (2007). Scaffolding and achievement in problem-based and inquiry learning: A response to Kirschner, Sweller, and Clark (2006). *Educational Psychologist, 42*(2), 99–107.

Hudson, P., Miller, S. P., & Butler, F. (2006). Adapting and merging explicit instruction within reform-based mathematics classrooms. *American Secondary Education, 35*(1), 19–32.

Hughes, L. (2002). *The collected works of Langston Hughes: The short stories.* Columbia: University of Missouri.

Hunter, M. C. (1976). *Improved instruction.* Thousand Oaks, CA: Corwin.

Jackson, R. (2009). *Never work harder than your students and other principles of great teaching.* Alexandria, VA: ASCD.

Jacobs, H. H. (2004). *Getting results with curriculum mapping.* Alexandria, VA: ASCD.

Jalajas, D. S., & Sutton, R. I. (1985) Feuds in student groups: Coping with whiners, martyrs, saboteurs, bullies, and deadbeats. *Organizational Behavior Teaching Review, 9*(4), 94–102.

Johnston, P. (2004). *Choice words: How our language affects children's learning.* York, ME: Stenhouse.

Justice, L. M. (2006). *Communication sciences and disorders: An introduction.* Upper Saddle River, NJ: Merrill/Prentice Hall.

Kanter, D. E. (2010). Doing the project and learning the content: Designing project-based science curricula for meaningful understanding. *Science Education, 94*(3), 525–551.

Kapur, M. (2008). Productive failure. *Cognition and Instruction, 26,* 379–424.

Kapur, M. (2009). Productive failure in mathematical problem solving. *Instructional Science, 36,* 523–550.

Kirschner, P. A., Sweller, J., & Clark, R. E. (2006). Why minimal guidance during instruction does not work: An analysis of constructivist, discovery, problem-based, experiential, and inquiry-based teaching. *Educational Psychologist, 41*(2), 75–86.

Kohn, A. (1999). *Punished by rewards: The trouble with gold stars, incentive plans, A's, praise, and other bribes.* Boston: Houghton Mifflin.

Lambert, J. (2002). *Digital storytelling: Capturing lives, creating community.* Berkeley, CA: Digital Diner.

Loewen, S., Li, S., Fei, F., Thompson, A., Nakatsukasa, K., Ahn, S., & Chen, X. (2009). Second language learners' beliefs about grammar instruction and error correction. *The Modern Language Journal, 93*(1), 91–104.

Luther, J. (2006). I-searching in context: Thinking critically about the research unit (p. 73). *English Journal, 95*(4), 68–74.

MacLeod, A. K., Tata, P., Tyrer, P., Schmidt, U., Davidson, K., & Thompson, S. (2005). Hopelessness and positive and negative future thinking in parasuicide. *British Journal of Clinical Psychology, 44*(4), 495–504.

Macrorie, K. (1988). The I-Search paper: Revised edition of searching writing. Portsmouth, NH: Boynton/Cook Heinemann.

Mager, R. F. (1962). *Preparing instructional objectives.* Belmont, CA: Fearon.

Marzano, R. J. (2009). *Designing and teaching learning goals and objectives.* Bloomington, IN: Solution Tree.

Marzano, R. J. (2011). Objectives that students understand. *Educational Leadership, 68*(8), 86–87.

Marzano, R. J., Pickering, D. J., & Pollock, J. E. (2001). *Classroom instruction that works: Research-based strategies for increasing student achievement.* Alexandria, VA: ASCD.

Masters, E. L. (1915). *Spoon River anthology.* New York: Macmillan.

Nation, I. S. P. (2001). *Vocabulary learning in another language.* Cambridge, England: Cambridge University Press.

National Governors Association Center for Best Practices and Council of Chief State School Officers. (2010). *Common core state standards.* Washington, DC: Author.

Naylor, P. R. (1992). *Shiloh.* New York: Atheneum.

Newmeyer, F. J. (2000). *Language form and language function.* Cambridge, MA: MIT Press.

Nuthall, G. (2005). The cultural myths and realities of classroom teaching and learning: A personal journey. *Teachers College Record, 107*(5), 895–934.

Ogle, D. M. (1986). K-W-L: A teaching model that develops active reading of expository text. *The Reading Teacher, 39,* 564–570.

Palumbo, T. J., & Willcutt, J. R. (2006). Perspectives on fluency: English-language learners and students with dyslexia. In S. J. Samuels & A. E. Farstrup (Eds.), *What research has to say about fluency instruction* (pp. 159–178). Newark, DE: International Reading Association.

Paris, S. G., Lipson, M., & Wixson, K. (1983). Becoming a strategic reader. *Contemporary Educational Psychology, 8,* 216–293.

Pearson, P. D., & Gallagher, M. C. (1983). The instruction of reading comprehension. *Contemporary Educational Psychology, 8,* 317–344.

Piper, W. (1930). *The little engine that could.* New York: Platt & Munk.

Prensky, M. (2001). Listen to the natives. *Educational Leadership, 63*(4), 8–13.

Raphael, T. E. (1986). Teaching question-answer relationships, revisited. *The Reading Teacher, 39,* 198–205.

Reiser, B. J., Tabak, I., Sandoval, W. A., Smith, B. K., Steinmuller, F., & Leone, A. J. (2001). BGuILE: Strategic and conceptual scaffolds for scientific inquiry in biology classrooms. In S. M. Carver & D. Klahr (Eds.), *Cognition and instruction: Twenty-five years of progress* (pp. 263–305). Mahwah, NJ: Erlbaum.

Rutter, M., Maughan, B., Mortimore, P., Ouston, J., & Smith, A. (1979). *Fifteen thousand hours: Secondary schools and their effects on children.* Cambridge, MA: Harvard University Press.

San Diego Unified School District. (2003, December 9). Cell phone and electronic signaling device policy, Board of Education approved Policy H-6980 [Online]. Retrieved from http://old.sandi.net:80/staff/principals/resources/articles/cell_policy.htm

Scarborough, H. S. (2001). Connecting early language and literacy to later reading (dis)abilities: Evidence, theory, and practice. In S. Neuman & D. Dickinson (Eds.), *Handbook for research in early literacy* (pp. 97–110). New York: Guilford Press.

Shepard, L. A. (2005). Linking formative assessment to scaffolding. *Educational Leadership, 63*(3), 66–70.

Sherin, B., Brown, M., & Edelson, D. C. (2005). On the content of task-structured science curricula. In L. B. Flick & N. Ledeman (Eds.), *Scientific inquiry and nature of science: Implications for teaching, learning, and teacher education.* Dordrecht, The Netherlands: Kluwer.

Shute, V. J. (2008). Focus on formative feedback. *Review of Educational Research, 78*(1), 153–189.

Simmons, J. (2003). Responders are taught, not born. *Journal of Adolescent and Adult Literacy, 46*(8), 684–693.

Stiggins, R. J., Arter, J., Chappuis, J., & Chappuis, S. (2004). *Classroom assessment for student learning: Doing it right—using it well.* Portland, OR: Assessment Training Institute.

Sullivan, G. S., & Strode, J. P. (2010). Motivation through goal setting: A self-determined perspective. *Strategies: A Journal for Physical and Sport Educators, 23*(6), 19–23.

Sweller, J. (1988). Cognitive load during problem solving: Effects on learning. *Cognitive Science, 12*(2), 257–285.

Sylvester, R., & Greenridge, W. (2009). Digital storytelling: Extending the potential for struggling writers. *The Reading Teacher, 63*(4), 284–295.

Tashjian, J. (1997). *Tru confessions.* New York: Squarefish.

Taylor, W. L. (1953). Cloze procedure: A new tool for measuring readability. *Journalism Quarterly, 30,* 415–433.

Topping, K. (2008). Peer assessment. *Theory into Practice, 48*(1), 20–27.

Vacca, R. T., & Vacca, J. L. (2007). *Content area reading: Literacy and learning across the curriculum* (9th ed.). Boston: Allyn & Bacon.

van den Bergh, L., Denessen, E., Hornstra, K., Voeten, M., & Holland, R. W. (2010). The implicit prejudiced attitudes of teachers: Relations to teacher expectations and the ethnic achievement gap. *American Educational Research Journal, 47*(2), 497–527.

Vygotsky, L. S. (1978). *Mind in society: The development of higher psychological processes.* Cambridge, MA: Harvard University Press.

Weaver, M. E. (1995). Using peer response in the classroom: Students' perspectives. *Research and Teaching in Developmental Education, 12,* 31–37.

White, B., & Johnson, T. S. (2001). We really do mean it: Implementing language arts standard #3 with opinionnaires. *The Clearing House, 74*(3), 119–123.

Wiggins, G. (1998). *Educative assessment: Designing assessments to inform and improve student performance.* San Francisco: Jossey-Bass.

Wiggins, G., & McTighe, J. (2005). *Understanding by design* (2nd ed.). Alexandria, VA: ASCD.

Index

Information in figures is indicated by *f*.

About the Authors

 **Douglas Fisher** is a professor of language and literacy education in the Department of Teacher Education at San Diego State University and a teacher leader at Health Sciences High & Middle College. He is a member of the California Reading Hall of Fame and is the recipient of a Celebrate Literacy Award from the International Reading Association, the Farmer Award for Excellence in Writing from the National Council of Teachers of English, and a Christa McAuliffe Award for Excellence in Teacher Education from the American Association of State Colleges and Universities. He has published numerous articles on improving student achievement, and his books include *Enhancing RTI: How to Ensure Success with Effective Classroom Instruction and Intervention, Checking for Understanding,* and *Content-Area Conversations.* He can be reached at dfisher@mail.sdsu.edu.

Nancy Frey is a professor of literacy in the School of Teacher Education at San Diego State University and a teacher leader at Health Sciences High & Middle College. Before joining the university faculty, Nancy was a special education teacher in the Broward County (Florida) Public Schools, where she taught students at the elementary and middle school levels. She later worked for the Florida Department of Education on a statewide project for supporting students with disabilities in a general education curriculum. Nancy is a recipient of the Christa McAuliffe Award for Excellence in Teacher Education from the American Association of State Colleges and Universities and the Early Career Award from the National Reading Conference. Her research interests include reading and literacy, assessment, intervention, and curriculum design. She has published many articles and books on literacy and instruction, including *Productive Group Work* and *Better Learning Through Structured Teaching*. She can be reached at nfrey@mail.sdsu.edu.